Get in The Game

GET

IN THE

GAME

By Bill Glass

WORD BOOKS

First Printing, October, 1965
Second Printing, November, 1965
Third Printing, December, 1965
Fourth Printing, July, 1966

WORD BOOKS • *Waco, Texas*

Dedication

To my Mother and my deceased Father who provided the home in which this boy and these ideas grew.

And to my Mother-in-law and Father-in-law who reared the girl I love most.

FOREWORD

This is a book of personal experience—of how a boy grows as a person, from sandlot football player to the top ranks of the professionals; and of how a Christian grows from his conversion experience to the marked degree of Christian maturity which Bill Glass shows in his everyday life.

This is a warm and human book encompassing Bill's experiences in his home, both as a child and as an adult with his own youngsters; his trials as a college and seminary student, his remarkable triumphs on the gridiron, as well as depression so serious it threatened his whole career.

This is a challenging book—a book which carries the straightforward Gospel message of hope and love which Bill Glass has witnessed to in countless meetings across the country. There is humor here, and Bill Glass is a master at retelling amusing incidents from a crucial play of a close game. There is triumph here—the triumph of the Risen Lord at work in Redeeming Love.

The section called "Pieces of Glass" is a noteworthy collection of anecdotes. Some of the observations are related to the sports field, but almost all may be aptly applied to life.

Bill Glass speaks frankly, and pulls no punches. But he knows young people—where they are and how they got that way.

BILLY GRAHAM

CONTENTS

PART I
OUT OF MY LIFE AND PLAY

PART II

PART III
LET'S PLAY THE GAME

INTRODUCTION

GET IN THE GAME! grew out of my feeling that too many Christians are still on the bench. Christians are too often spectators and aren't really participants in the thick of the battle. Paul said, "I don't shadow box, I really fight." He's saying, "I'm not just playing church, I'm in a real fight to the death."

While it is largely addressed to teens and young adults, I pray that this effort will be helpful in showing to people of all ages a whole new way of life.

To be honest, the biographical section was done primarily as an afterthought. And then, only at the insistence of friends.

I must express appreciation to those friends who encouraged me to write this book: James Dunn, Billy Zeoli, Wayne Philpott, Bill Anderson, Jarrell McCracken, and my most wonderful friend, Sam Bender; and to professors who made great contributions to my life: Dr. Jack MacGorman, Dr. Kenneth Chafin, Dr. T. B. Maston, Dr. Cal Guy, Dr. Milton Fergeson, Dr. H. C. Brown, Dr. William Hendricks (all of Southwestern Baptist Theological Seminary, a great place primarily because of them); from Baylor days, the big three were: Dr. W. J. Wimpee, Dr. George Stokes, and Dr. Kyle Yates.

Appreciation is due, similarly, to coaches who have made vital contributions to my athletic career: Bill Stages, Sam Boyd, Don Shula, Blanton Collier, Nick Skorich, Vernon Glass (my brother, who has inspired and instructed me and who is also a coach); and teammates too numerous to name; and to Larry Walker, the college friend who challenged me to be more than a second-rate football player.

Part I

OUT OF MY LIFE
AND PLAY

CHAPTER ONE

How Did It Happen?

With four games still to play, we, the Cleveland Browns, thought we had clinched our division championship for the 1964 season. Then we were beaten 28 to 21 by the Green Bay Packers. The next week we played Washington and won 38 to 24, but the following week St. Louis gave us a terrible beating, 28 to 19. This left us half a game in front with New York still to be played. We had to win over New York in order to clinch the division championship and play Baltimore for the World's Championship. The pressure was really on. New York had not had a good year, but they were still a good team. The first half was close, but then the game broke wide-open and we went on to win by a score of 52 to 20. We won our division but we had fought for our lives down to the very last.

Baltimore had won their division with four games left to play. They knew that they were going to be playing for the World's Championship a full month before we

did. They had developed a spirit of complacency. The
uncertainty of our division championship had left us
sharp and ready to go. We thought that we had a good
chance of beating Baltimore.

No sports writer in America had picked us to win
except our own sports writer Chuck Heaton of the
Cleveland *Plain Dealer*. Vince Costello and I told him
laughingly before the game that the reason he picked us
was because if we lost everyone would say,

"Well, Chuck had to pick his own team," but if we
won people would say,

"Chuck is a football prophet."
Every other sports writer picked the powerful Balti-
more with the great Johnny Unitas as quarterback and
Raymond Berry as the receiving end.

I knew as a defensive end that if our line gave Unitas
time to pass he'd run us out of the park. In the first half
I was double teamed. In other words, the offensive end
and tackle had teamed up to block me. I had never in
my career faced an offensive end and tackle both blocking me on a pass play. Normally on a pass play an
offensive end will go down field. Baltimore's offensive
slot-end stayed in and blocked me along with the tackle.
I think this tactic hurt Baltimore more than it helped
them. It cut down on the number of men that they had
in the pass patterns, allowing us to cover some of their
better receivers like Berry and Lennie Moore with two
men. In the third quarter they stopped double teaming
me and sent their slot-end out into the pattern. Since
I was blocked by only one man, I was able to help put
pressure on Johnny Unitas. Our offense, led by Frank
Ryan, Gary Collins, and Jim Brown, was great. And

who would have imagined that our defense could have
held that great Baltimore offense scoreless? We shut out
Baltimore by a score of 27 to 0 to win the World's
Championship before a crowd of 80,000 people.

My wife Mavis had been at this championship game.
Immediately after the game we drove home, picked up
our children, packed our car, said good-by to all our
neighbors, and left for home via Chicago. I had to be in
Chicago at 11 o'clock the next morning to speak to a
large youth convention in a downtown hotel. We ar-
rived there about 4 o'clock that morning, checked in,
and got a few hours sleep. At 9 o'clock I was at the convention. I conferred with Billy Zeoli, president of Youth
Films and a close friend. He briefed me on the nature of
the audience, telling me that many of the young people
there were Christians, but there were also many who
were not. It would be important for me to address my
remarks both to Christians and non-Christians. I talked
to the young people about the importance of standing
for that which is really worthwhile in life. The heart of
my message was that Jesus Christ is the most worthwhile
thing in life to stand for. The major portion of my
message dealt with the reasons why I believe that only
Jesus Christ is worth the first allegiance in our lives. At
the conclusion of my message, I offered an invitation to
the young people to trust Christ as the Lord of their
lives or to make a public decision in some special way.
Many of the young people responded. They came forward and went into a room where the leaders of the
convention were able to counsel with them.

A world's championship football game and a procla-
mation of the good news of Jesus Christ were almost

simultaneous events in the life of the same person. How could this be? How did I happen to be doing both things at the same time? Well, both vocations have their roots in my childhood. For years I have known that God has wanted me in two places at the same time—on the gridiron and in the pulpit.

CHAPTER TWO

Sandlot, and Lots More

I have been interested in football as long as I can remember. My brother Vernon, seven years older than I am, was always my ideal. Whatever he said was true, was right, and was law for me. He was one of the finest athletes in our city of Corpus Christi, Texas. I tried to follow his footsteps and live up to the reputation that he had built as an athlete in school. He was my hero. Vernon was an all-state quarterback on the high school football team.

As a boy I thoroughly enjoyed playing sandlot football. I played constantly through the years that I was in grade school. I played football with the rest of the neighborhood kids in a big field out by our house. We had some fierce contests. We didn't wear equipment, but we tackled full speed, hitting as hard as we possibly could. We had a great time.

The first time that I became aware of my inherent love for contact sports and physical prowess was in grade school. I had been a schoolyard scrapper since I was in the third or fourth grade. I had never been a bully or picked a fight, but it was recognized by the rest of the kids on the schoolyard that I was one of the toughest kids in school. I gained a reputation; and like a "wild west" gun slinger I had to fight almost daily. Every other kid in school felt the obligation to fight me sooner or later. Every kid wanted to be considered tougher than everyone else and, of course, this always led to challenge matches. We weren't big or tough enough to really hurt each other, but we did have a great time wrestling and scrapping together. On the last day of school in the sixth grade I was helping my teacher. With me in the room were three or four other boys assisting the teacher. One of the boys implied to the teacher that I was tough and that I was a good wrestler. Because I had always been quiet and unobstrusive in the classroom, the teacher was surprised and shocked by my reputation as a fighter. She said,

"Why, you don't mean that Bill would fight, do you?" And they said,

"Oh, yes, he fights almost every day." My teacher just couldn't accept it. She later told my mother that she couldn't believe that I would ever fight. In junior high school I became a "peace lover" when I discovered that the fellows were so much bigger and tougher than I.

I always think of my childhood home as an affectionate one. My father displayed his love for my mother and for the children openly. I can remember my parents always kissed me goodnight. Dad was a good provider—we lived in a nice home and drove a nice automobile. We were always a very close family.

One day our home life took on an additional quality. My father's best friend, a neighbor, became a Christian. My Dad was amazed at the change that had come over his friend. He said,

"If Christ can help Obie Grief, then certainly the Christian faith can add new meaning to my life."

My father, attending church with our neighbor, came to find Christ as his Lord. As a result of this genuine conversion, he began to live as a Christian. I knew my father before and after his conversion to Christianity and I saw the new dimension that Christ gave to him. His conversion made our home into a wonderful place in which to live. I lived with the experience of my father's conversion to Christ all during my childhood days. It left such a vivid memory with me that I was never able to forget it.

When I was in grade school I was a fairly good athlete. I was agile and fast on my feet. When I went to junior high school I began to grow fast. I became very clumsy. I was not oversized; I was about the same size as other boys my age, but I developed unusually big hands and big feet. I was like a puppy that has overgrown paws and overgrown ears; the rest of his body hasn't caught up yet.

Since my brother had played quarterback, I decided that this was the position for me to play when I went to junior high school. But I made a terrible quarterback. I had two left feet and two left hands and I couldn't possibly play effectively in this position. The coaches quickly moved me to the guard position. I never made first string in junior high school and played little in the games. It was not until I was a sophomore in high school that I began to play consistently in the games and with the first string.

Between my sophomore and junior years in high school I grew very rapidly. I grew from 150 pounds to 190 pounds and picked up several inches in height. I was slowly becoming more agile than I had formerly been. During my junior year in high school, I decided that I was going to make the first string in football if it was the last thing I did. To carry out this resolve, I became more violent in my blocking. One day in scrimmage I hit the guy across the line from me as hard as I could. To my amazement, I knocked him flat on his back. I was so impressed that I decided that this was the way to play football—to make it a tough contact sport. It worked. My coaches were impressed, and I consistently played first string ball after I threw myself into the game with this new gusto.

But even though I was on the first string I gradually came to recognize that something was missing in my life. I was sixteen, but I had never been deeply involved in the life of my church. My father had become a Christian in a Baptist church and therefore I was interested in the same church. Yet I had not accepted Christ as Lord. In a casual way, I knew some of the church young people who attended school with me. I knew that they had a quality of life which I didn't have. My interest in their Christian life grew over a period of months. I began to imitate their behavior, but copying their actions wasn't enough to satisfy the spiritual hunger that I was experiencing.

One Sunday morning in November during my junior year in high school, I attended church. I was sitting about a third of the way back in the congregation during the worship service. My moral and spiritual unrest had reached a climax. The conviction grew with me during the preaching hour that I must make a decision to accept Christ. During the invitation at the close of the worship service, I made my commitment to Christ as Lord. I felt that if I didn't make this decision I would physically, mentally, and spiritually explode. A great burden was lifted from my shoulders and a new dimension of life opened up before me.

I had been a member of the church since I was twelve years old, but I had never come to know Christ as the Lord of my life before this November Sunday morning. I felt quite hypocritical because I knew that I had never really experienced a relationship to God in my heart. In reflecting on this experience from the perspective of later years, I know that it was a commitment of my whole person to God in Christ. It involved my will, my emotions, and my intellect. I knew that I needed Christ as Savior; I wanted to accept Him as the Lord of my life; and I wanted to enter into a relationship with God, my heavenly Father. This is what I did.

Early in my Christian experience, I came to depend upon the Scripture. I committed portions of it to memory. Some of the meaningful verses to me in these early days were John 6:37, "Him that cometh unto me I will in no wise cast out"; Romans 10:13, "For whosoever shall call upon the name of the Lord shall be saved"; and First John 5:10-15, which gives us assurance that if we do His will, He hears our prayers and answers them.

As a young Christian, I knew very little about how

to behave as a Christian. I had gone to Sunday School spasmodically, but I had little background training and knowledge of the Scripture or church life. Yet I was eager to learn and to grow. With the help of a wonderful pastor, I quickly came to know some of the meaning of the Christian life.

In the spring of this same junior year in high school a youth evangelist, Browning Ware, came to our church. Browning was a very able speaker. I had planned to attend every evening meeting after football practice. I was in the shower after workout early one evening with a couple of my teammates. These guys were top players on our team. One of them said to me,

"What are you going to do tonight, Bill?" I said,

"Well, I'm going to church."

"Oh, really?"

"Yes, you ought to come with me." I didn't expect them to say,

"O. K.",

but they did. Later they told me they came just for kicks. They didn't have anything else to do and they just wanted to see what it was all about. They had noticed a change in my life and this stimulated their interest. They went with me to the service that night. After the evening message, one of them said to me,

"You know, if someone had told me a little bit more, I would have publicly responded to the message at the end of the service."

Seeing this as an opportunity I tried to describe to them what the Christian life was all about. I told them everything that I knew and some things that I didn't know. I still knew so little about the Christian life that I shared with them everything that I knew in about fifteen minutes. At home that night I telephoned Browning Ware, the revival speaker, and asked him if he would help in talking to these young athletes. He said that he would, and the next day he talked with both of them. As a result they came to know Christ and had a wonderful conversion experience.

Because of the public commitment of these two athletes to Christ and the Christian faith, young people in our high school became interested in these revival services. Before the week was over, a number of the players on our football team and a great many other high school young people came to know Christ as a result of hearing about Him in this revival. This experience whetted my appetite for sharing Christ with other people, but I still didn't know how to go about it. I didn't know how to lead anyone to Christ myself. Yet I began to talk to my high school friends and encouraged them to be Christians. I looked upon conversion to the Christian faith as a delicate spiritual operation. I thought it could be performed only by the finest of specialists. I knew that I was no such specialist, but I felt that my pastor was. I began to bring my friends to talk with my pastor about becoming a Christian, and many of them came to know Christ in this way. By listening to him talk with my friends, I, too, found deeper meaning in my faith. By observing him, I learned how to lead other people to Christ.

For about a year I brought my friends, both my age and younger, to talk with my pastor, Dr. Warren Walker. Finally he said to me,

"Bill, you know I really enjoy talking about the Lord

with these people that you bring to me. I think it's wonderful that you do this. I hate to tell you to stop, but I would like for you to have the joy of leading them all the way through to conversion yourself."

Up to this point I had merely pointed my friends to Christ and shown them their need of Him, but I had always let my pastor lead them into the conversion experience. Now my pastor was encouraging me to assume that role. He knew that I would soon be going away to college and that he would no longer be available when I needed him. I had gained enough knowledge from listening to him to know how to do this. So with his encouragement, I began to talk to people and to lead them all the way to Christ.

During my senior year in high school, I weighed 210 pounds and was 6'4" in height. My agility was improving slowly and I was gaining a little speed in my running. I was not an outstanding football player, but it looked as if I had potential for the college years ahead. My size alone apparently impressed the college coaches. Every Southwest Conference football team invited me to come to play football for them on a full scholarship. I realized that these invitations came not because I was such a great high school football player, but because it looked as if I might develop in college. My brother's reputation may also have been a factor. He had established himself as a fine quarterback at Rice Institute and was one of the best quarterbacks in Southwest Conference football.

That senior year I faced a critical decision. Should I accept a scholarship to Rice where my brother had played football or should I go to another Southwest Conference school? Because my brother had been at

Rice I had fallen in love with that school. My father, mother, and I had made the trip to Houston for every home game for four years. I loved Rice; I knew the school song; I had spent a lot of time in the dormitories; I knew all the football players, the trainers, and the coaches. Coach Neely had talked to me about going to Rice. Coach Joe Davis, the line coach, and Coach Charlie Moore, the freshman coach, had talked to me about playing on the Rice team. My brother Vernon was eager for me to follow in his footsteps, but he said,

"It's your own decision to make and I'm not going to tell you where to go to school. It's four years of your own life."

I had been so enthusiastic about going to Rice that I had sold the rest of the players on our high school team on going there. There were seven players on our team who had been offered Southwest Conference scholarships and I talked five of them into going to Rice with me. And yet I decided to go to Baylor University, in Waco, Texas.

I had visited every Southwest Conference school. I loved Rice like I loved no other school. But I knew that I was just a beginner as a Christian; I felt that I needed the influence of a Christian school in order to grow spiritually. Having visited Baylor's campus, I sensed that there I might find the best nurture and encouragement in my Christian life. I was most impressed with the distinctively Christian atmosphere among faculty and students. I made this final decision a real object of prayer. I finally came to feel that Baylor was the school that could offer what I needed for spiritual growth.

Among my high school friends I still talked about

going to Rice, but I had already made the decision deep down in my heart about enrolling at Baylor. My teammates who had decided to go to Rice because I had so influenced them really gave me a hard time when they found out that I wasn't going with them. I took a great deal of kidding from them at that time and to this day when I see them, they still rib me about the fact that I influenced them to go to one school and then I turned around and went to another.

CHAPTER THREE

College Days:

All-American and All That

That fall I went to Baylor with the desire to be as effective a football player as I could possibly be. I remember the first day we were out to scrimmage the varsity. They were big. I weighed only about 210 pounds. I was playing the defensive middle guard. I was scared; they ran a few plays and I made a few tackles. I thought I was doing fairly well for a freshman, but then the varsity ran a wedge play. This play is designed to remove all pesky middle guards. In the wedge play the center hits the middle guard as hard as he can. Then both guards and both tackles hit him. Finally both ends hit him. Then each back tries to step on the middle guard if possible. Pretty soon the middle guard gets the feeling that he's on a one-way street going the wrong way. Everyone wants to step on him. I have discovered that the best thing to do on the wedge play is to hit the ground and hope that someone will trip over you.

There were some days when it was really tough playing football as a freshman, but I began to feel more and more confident in playing the game. I got bigger and faster. I became more agile; I could keep my balance, and I developed an understanding of the game as well as more confidence in playing it.

One thing that helped me in making the Baylor football team was something that I had learned to do in high school. This was the "one-on-one" drill, the basic drill for linemen taught to me by my football coach in high school, Bill Stages. Coach Stages showed me the basic importance of controlling the blocker—both his head and his shoulders. He taught me to control the head and shoulders of the blocker, never letting him get blocking position on me. Having learned this lesson in high school, I did very well as a freshman at Baylor in my first days on the team when we had the "one-on-one" drill. In college football during scrimmage and during the games, I was able to control the blocker. This apparently impressed the coaches and helped me to make the team. I became the middle guard on the five-man line. (The five-man line with the middle guard over the center was the predominant defense in college football at that time.) I established myself as a middle guard because I controlled the center's head and fought through him to the play.

During spring training in my freshman year, in preparation for sophomore football, we were visited by Steve Owen. For years Owen was head coach for the New York Giants and one of the great pro coaches of all time. For the few weeks of spring training he acted as an advisor. At the end of the spring he indicated that I was the best pro football prospect on the ball club. I was stunned. My teammates were shocked. No one on the club thought that I had a future in football. His cheering words were of great encouragement to me. I was fighting the problem of confidence in myself at this time because I still did not have the proper balance and the speed for first-class college football.

When I was a sophomore, Baylor played the University of Washington. At that time, I weighed 215 pounds. I had to play right over their tackle who weighed 260 pounds. The game was well under way when their tackle became very angry at me. He came up from the ground and hit me in the teeth and tried to rearrange the way I ate. To say that I wanted to do something illegal in return would be the understatement of the year. When I told our coach about it on the side-lines, he pointed out several good reasons why I could not lose my sense of control and punch the tackle in the mouth. I might get kicked out of the game; I might cost my team a fifteen yard penalty; I might miss my block or tackle that was necessary to help my team win the game. I had a hard time holding myself under control; but I discovered that my coach was right. The best way to get back at an illegal player is to play the game legally as hard as you can. This was one of the lessons that I learned as a sophomore and it has helped me all the way through my football career. A player who loses his poise always hurts his team. The essence of good football is to concentrate on carrying out the details of your assignment on every play. To lose your poise is to break your concentration.

Baylor University is a Baptist school. Many of the Baptist churches in the vicinity wanted the Christian athletes on our team to come to the churches to tell about their Christian lives. I got many opportunities to give my Christian testimony. I spoke in different churches in the surrounding cities with a great sense of joy. My talks became so lengthy that a friend suggested that I might as well call them sermons since I was speaking so long. I took him at his word and began to preach.

Many people have asked me when I first felt God's call to enter the Christian ministry. I think of myself as a lay minister rather than as an ordained minister. I have never been ordained or licensed to preach. I can point to no specific time when God called me into the lay ministry. I became more and more aware of God's presence as I continued to speak in various churches and assemblies. When I finally worked up to a full-length sermon, I had many opportunities for week-end youth meetings. Between my sophomore and junior years I had graduated to full week meetings, and I began speaking at summer assemblies. In fact, I traveled all over the United States in revival meetings that summer.

I was a layman, but I felt that God was leading me to these speaking engagements. Many of these doors were opened as a result of my football career. As I gained ability and confidence in playing football, more opportunities were granted to me to speak in different parts of the country. I filled as many of these engagements as I could.

During my first two years in college I met with different Christian athletes to study the Bible. Between ten and twenty-five of us would get together in the dormitory to discuss the Bible, read it, and pray together. We did this about once a week. These meetings were very helpful to us. We would discuss our doubts, our victories, our defeats, and share our problems. Sometimes our fellow athletes who were not Christians would attend these meetings. They were interested in and impressed with what we said and discussed there. They continued to come to the meetings. Often we were able to show them more about the Christian life.

In college I began to realize the importance of motivation in playing football. I became aware that when I played well on the field, it impressed my teammates and made them ready to listen to what I had to say off the field. Coaches, alumni, and friends are more impressed by a good football player than they are by a mediocre player. They are more eager to hear what a good player has to say. This growing awareness motivated me to play better and to give football everything I had. I wanted to have an audience for what I had to say concerning the Christian faith. I realized that I didn't have much of an edge over anyone in football except for a psychological edge which I wanted to develop. I feel that this motivation was one of the things that goaded me on to being an effective football player as a senior in college.

The first season game of my senior year in college was scheduled to be played on the West Coast. A few days before this game a close friend and fellow student and I got together. He was a football enthusiast and a dedicated Christian. He told me something that I already knew.

"Bill, you're only an average football player, but you could be worlds better. If you are outstanding in your

senior year there will be added opportunities for you to
have an influence for Christ."

He continued,

"You have the physical equipment to be a great football player. God would widen your Christian testimony
as a result of it. You've been playing fairly good football so far, and all your coaches are relatively pleased.
But honestly, Bill, you've just been mediocre. So, if you
play inspired football your senior year, amazing things
can happen."

My friend and I began to make this goal a real object
of prayer. Three days before we were to go to the West
Coast to play the University of California, we were in
prayer. He became so bold as to say,

"Let's pray specifically that you may become an All-
American and that as an All-American, you may use
whatever glory this honor brings you to the glory of
God."

During this prayer meeting we had a peculiar awareness of God's presence. With these challenging thoughts
and convictions before us, we rose to our feet with the
realization that something big might happen.

Three days later when we played the University of
California, my play was better than it had ever been
before. I was making tackles and doing things in the
game that I had never done before. I was playing with
my whole heart and everything I had was given to the
game. As the game progressed, I found myself tackling
runners whom I thought were fake men who turned out
to be actually carrying the ball. I was stumbling into
more things than I normally would have done by trying
hard. After the game was over, I discovered, to my

amazement, that I had made seventeen unassisted tackles. I had done more in that one ball game than I had ever done in any other ball game in my entire life. This set a pattern for my play throughout my senior year.

The next week we played on the East Coast against the University of Maryland and the following week we played in Nebraska against the University of Nebraska. Within three weeks we played before the sports writers in the West, East, and Midwest. We were exposed to most of the sports writers of the country and they were the ones who would make the decisions concerning the All-American team. Everything during my senior year seemed to work together to make it possible for me to become an All-American.

I had never thought about being an All-American until this senior year in college, but then it became my goal. After my friend had challenged me, I felt that it was imperative that I be as good a player as I possibly could be. If I were not, I would let my team down; but more important I would lose an opportunity for a Christian witness. My goal during my senior year was to play inspired football.

To be named to the All-American team was my secret goal for my entire senior year. I had been praying and working for this victory. At the end of the football year, the head coach called me into his office. He said, "Bill, I think you know what I am going to tell you."

Still, when he told me that I had really made it, it was something of a shock. Making the All-American team has always been a source of strength to me because I feel that it was a direct answer to prayer. I had never had this kind of ability and had never played this quality of football. I was shocked and pleased and thankful to God.

My coach shared this news with me two or three weeks before it became public. The day the news was made public, newspaper and radio people came out to the practice. I was interviewed by the newsmen right after the practice session. I asked Coach Sam Boyd, our head coach, what I should say. He said,

"You should give credit to your teammates and then whatever else you feel you'd like to say."

I'll never forget the credits that I gave. I said,

"I feel that I owe a great deal to my teammates. I owe much to my fine coaches—Sam Boyd, our head coach, Hardin Cooper our line coach, and Steve Owen, who has helped me greatly here at Baylor University. Bill Stages, my high school coach, set me on the right path; but more than anyone else, I owe a debt to the One who has made us and all of this possible, God."

After I had made All-American it seemed that everyone in Texas and the Southwest began to call inviting me to speak in schools, churches, clubs, and in every type of organization. Every time I received a phone call I would hear, ringing in my ears, the words I had said and the promises I had made to God—that if I was effective in my senior year as an athlete I would give the glory to Him. I wanted to use all of these speaking opportunities as best as I could for God's glory. The speaking task ahead almost overwhelmed me.

At Baylor I had made many B's, some A's, and a few C's. I had studied fairly hard all during my football career, but when the opportunities for speaking started coming I felt obligated to accept every one of them that

I could. Speaking at all these places became physically impossible because there were many opportunities. Yet I did accept at least one speaking engagement for every night throughout the spring. I think I had four or five nights off all spring. I spent much of the spring traveling over the state of Texas speaking at football banquets, church banquets, and youth rallies. I felt obligated to take advantage of this new-found athletic popularity for God's glory. But my grades suffered a great deal. I ended up making all C's that last semester at Baylor. I have often wondered if I did not take my promise to God too literally. I believe that it was God's will for me to take these speaking engagements, but I realize now that it was just as much His will for me to study harder and prepare myself fully for the years ahead.

I always find it difficult to turn down an opportunity to speak about Christ. One of the biggest dilemmas that I have ever faced is telling people "No" when invited to speak. That spring of my senior year, I felt that I should accept every opportunity that I got. I got so many that I finally had to draw the line somewhere because it was running me down physically. I had weighed 230 pounds when the season was over, but by the end of the spring, I was down to 215 pounds. I was literally worn out but still getting more opportunities than I could possibly accept. I finally realized that the only sane thing to do was to limit myself to what I could adequately handle.

One group I really enjoyed talking to that year was a big group of boys. Before the final game of my college career I was scheduled to go to the auditorium at Baylor to speak to a group of Royal Ambassadors (a youth organization in the Baptist church). These kids were from the age of nine to fourteen or fifteen. There were five thousand of them crammed into the auditorium when I spoke to them. After this assembly they all went to the game. For this game (with Rice) the coaches had moved me from the middle guard position to the linebacker position. On one play I faded back for a pass coverage. The Rice quarterback threw the pass; I jumped into the air and barely tipped the ball with my fingers. The ball was deflected, bounced straight up in the air, and came down in my hands. I caught it and ran about forty-five yards toward the goal line. It looked as if I were going to score when two Rice players knocked me out of bounds on the three-yard line. That's the closest I ever came to scoring in my senior year. When I intercepted the ball, I ran in the direction of the stands where the five thousand Royal Ambassadors were seated. All five thousand of them let out a tremendous yell—the loudest yelling I have ever heard. After the game many of them told me that they thought I had intercepted the pass and run in their direction specifically for them. I had talked with them before the game and they felt that they were closely identified with me. In reality, I caught the ball by accident and ran out of sheer fright because I had so seldom handled the ball as a college football player.

During my years as a Christian in high school I had a great deal of zeal for the cause of Christ. I thought that the world could be won for Christ immediately and I wanted to be in the center of this effort. I intended to do a great deal of this winning myself; and in my own strength rather than letting the Lord work through me to accomplish His purpose. Zeal without knowledge would characterize my activity at that time. When someone asked me to speak or give a testimony, I jumped at the opportunity and spoke loud and long. There was nothing wrong with this type of enthusiasm. I think that young Christians should be zealous. It would be wonderful if older Christians could have some of the zeal of new Christians. I feel that zeal without knowledge is better than knowledge without zeal. Knowledge and zeal together offer an effective combination which can do a great deal in the service of God.

Throughout my freshman and sophomore years at Baylor, I continued to view my Christian life through rose-colored glasses. I felt that everything was wonderful and that there were no serious problems to be experienced. Disillusionment was unknown to me. By the time I was a junior at Baylor I had experienced both disillusionment and times of discouragement. While taking courses in the Philosophy Department at Baylor, I was introduced to many new ideas that strained my faith. As a Christian I had not faced many of the live and vital problems of philosophy. Upon first contact with these philosophical problems, my zeal for Christ cooled off and I was discouraged.

Some of the serious questions that I faced for the first time were,

"Is God really a good God?

"Why does God permit evil and suffering in the world?

"What is the ultimate fate of those who have never heard of Christ?

"What is man's source of authority?

"Is the Bible reliable?

"Is the Scripture the authentic word of God?"

I remember one of my professors in a religion course pointing to a huge map of the world and saying,

"What if you were born in Asia? Would you still be a Christian? Since there are so many different religions in the world, how do you know that Christianity is unique as opposed to the rest of these religions? How do you know that Christ is right and Mohammed is wrong?"

These questions posed real difficulties for me intellectually. They were not fully answered for me while I was in college. It was not until theological seminary and further studies that I gained satisfying intellectual answers to them.

My zeal for Christ was restored through the constant remembrance of the very real and vivid conversion I had experienced in high school, the realization of God's presence in my life, and the answers to prayer that I continued to have. My experience in prayer before the first game during my senior year left an indelible impression on me. The way that God blessed in my playing on the field rekindled my loyalty to Christ. I would not have missed facing these intellectual problems for anything; wrestling with them strengthened me and helped dispel my doubts and turmoils. These questions broadened both my intellectual and spiritual horizons. They ultimately strengthened my faith and experiences in Christ.

During my high school years I dated some, but football kept me so busy I just didn't have time to "go out" a lot. It was different when I got to college. My interest in girls accelerated. I dated twelve or fifteen different girls, but I never seriously contemplated marrying any of them. The first time, I guess, that I really thought seriously about marriage was during my senior year. I had a very idealistic view of marriage. I felt that my future wife would be a Christian, that we would have a great deal in common, and that she would be a wonderful person. I don't know why, but I thought she'd be a freshman. I knew that marriage would be a serious step and I made it a matter of prayer . . . not constantly, of course, for I didn't think I was that close to it, but there were many times when I did ask God to have His will about who I dated and ultimately married.

I heard by the campus grapevine that Mavis Knapp, a cute little brunette (a freshman, by the way) wanted to meet me. I thought that she must be out of her head and I really didn't feel that anything would come of it. But if she really wanted to date me, and if she were as cute as they said, I couldn't see any reason why I shouldn't accommodate her. A mutual friend introduced us, and we had our first date. Actually I was going out to preach at North Waco Baptist Church, so I asked Mavis if she could sing or play the piano. I figured if she were going along she might as well be of some use. I took her with me, anyway, even though she could do neither. I thought she was hilarious. She was Homecoming Queen nominee that year, and on our second date I escorted her to one of the functions. Right off, she told me that she felt she wanted to marry a person like me. I was amazed and thought,

"I really picked a dumb freshman this time."

But she was so sparkling I continued to date her. I

soon learned that she was really sincere in what she felt to be God's leadership. If God had initiated her interest in someone like me, who was I to argue? As we continued to date, I continued to seek God's will for our friendship. I began to feel that God had destined us for each other, but I didn't know why. How was I to know that she was to be the greatest thing that ever happened to me?

I have often looked back in wonder at why I had the growing certainty that the relationship between Mavis and me was a part of God's plan for our lives. From the very beginning, although we knew little about each other, we sensed that we shared much in common. As we continued to date, we discovered these areas of mutual agreement. Her background was the same as mine. She was converted to a vital faith in Christ when she was 15. Her parents were both from east Texas, as were mine, and they had both moved to south Texas when we were quite young. Her parents had moved to Harlingen in the Rio Grande Valley before she was born. My parents had moved to Corpus Christi when I was about four years old. Each summer we had both gone to small towns in east Texas for vacation—she, to Hearne in Central east Texas, and I to Bloomburg. Her mother's family were farm people and very dedicated Christians, as were my mother's people. Both our maternal grandparents maintained strong family ties. Our departures from our grandparents after these summer vacations were always hard for us, and often ended in tears. Dad's people were also Christians and had a strong cultural background as did hers. Grandfather was a district judge for a number of years in east Texas. My

uncle was a district attorney. Mavis and I were not fully
fully aware of our similarities in background, yet we
knew that we were a great deal alike in many respects.

Mavis told some of her college friends that she was
going to marry me. Of course, they thought this was a
great joke. She cut my picture out of the football program and put it on the mirror in her room. Marriage to
me became a goal for her. I later wondered why she had
such a poor goal. At any rate, this was her goal, and she
achieved it a lot quicker than she ever thought she
would. She was the one who engineered our first meeting, but I removed every obstacle in her way after that.
Somehow, she was certain of our marriage long before
I even realized that she was seriously interested in me.
We became engaged three months after our first date.

After the game with Rice during my senior year, I
drove to Harlingen and took an engagement ring for
Mavis with me. Her parents gave us a huge engagement
party at their home. I'd been so tied up getting to know
Mavis I hadn't thought much about her family. She sure
had a big one. I met them all. Her dad has four brothers
and five sisters. Each one of them has a big family. I just
couldn't remember everyone's name. There were so
many different people that I couldn't keep everybody
straight. The only comfortable thing about the engagement party was that I got a crack at them first in a
formal preaching service before they got a shot at me
at the engagement party.

I spoke at the First Baptist Church there in Harlingen
on Sunday night just before the engagement party. As I
walked down the aisle of the church with the pastor, I
glanced to my right and was startled to see my future

father-in-law sitting with a strange woman. I thought to
myself,

"What kind of family am I getting into?"

Sitting at the front of the church with the pastor, I
glanced to the left of the auditorium and saw my future
father-in-law sitting with his wife. I thought to myself.

"He sure made a quick switch; this time he's sitting
with his wife."

Looking back to the right of the auditorium, I saw
him again sitting with the strange woman. Then I realized for the first time that he had an identical twin
brother. There was a big crowd for the service. Most of
them, I guess, were part of Mavis' very large family.

Three months later on March 2, 1957, Mavis and I
were married at that same church. There were 1200
people in attendance. We had a wonderful reception
afterwards at the country club, with people from all
over the Rio Grande Valley attending. We went to
Brownsville, a Texas-Mexico border city, for a real short
honeymoon.

I was still very conscious of my pact with God, about
speaking for Him whenever I could. So, after only two
days in Brownsville, Mavis and I flew to Kansas City
and went out to William Jewel College campus for their
Religious Emphasis Week. We spent the rest of our
honeymoon speaking on the campus, and enduring a
barrage of good-natured kidding from those college
students. They knew that we were on our honeymoon.
I had not yet graduated from college and Mavis was
still a freshman. We were about the same age as most of
them. Somehow, though, I think that helped us establish
contact which we might not have otherwise enjoyed.

After that, Mavis thought that she had married a whirlwind rather than a husband. For the first three months of our marriage we went from one speaking engagement to another. Up until the time she married me, Mavis had led a very quiet and rather sheltered life. This was completely different. I knew that she was in complete sympathy with my reasons for speaking every night, but the tremendous pace and all of the traveling wasn't good for either of us. After that things seemed to slow down a bit although Mavis says,

"Sure . . . we went from a whirlwind to a tornado."

I think the Lord takes care of fools and idiots because Mavis and I have had the happiest marriage of anybody I know. We did have a very short engagement period, but I certainly wouldn't suggest short engagements for others. The longer engagement you have and the longer you take to get to know each other, the better chance you have for a successful marriage. Young couples who enter into short engagements can't always be certain that they will be blessed with as happy a marriage as Mavis and I have had.

Mavis is an ardent football fan. She enthusiastically follows every game most of the time from the stands. She is my greatest rooter. I often tease her by telling her that when I first went into pro football she was terrified at the possibility of my being injured. She was always solicitous over the smallest injury and quite sympathetic. I tell her that since she has learned to enjoy the money and other benefits of pro football she minimizes my injuries, and that every time I receive the slightest injury she is afraid that I will quit pro ball.

CHAPTER FOUR

The Ups and Downs
of a Defensive End

When I graduated from Baylor University, I faced another hard decision. I felt that the Lord wanted me to continue to prepare myself academically for some form of Christian service. Although I was not an ordained minister, the most obvious thing for me to do would be to pursue a theological education. At the same time, I had opportunities to play professional football. How could I continue a theological education and play professional football at the same time?

I had been the first draft choice of the Detroit Lions in the National Football League. The Saskatchewan Rough Riders of the Canadian Football League also drafted me. Several of my Baylor teammates were playing for the Rough Riders. Jack Russell, our head line coach at Baylor, had influenced us to play for the Rough Riders. Because of this influence I felt that I should play in Canada my first year in pro ball. When I went to play in Canada, Detroit was very unhappy with me.

The Rough Riders and their supporters had high expectations as to what I could contribute to their ball club. I had been an All-American, the first draft choice of Detroit, and also their first draft choice. I was front page news on the Regina Saskatchewan newspaper where the ball club was located. Three weeks before I went to Canada, that newspaper started a count-down of the remaining weeks before I would arrive. During the last week before I got there, the newspaper had a front page day-by-day countdown—seven days, six days, five days, four days, three days, two days, one day. I had the feeling of an astronaut returning to home base. But both my hope and their hopes were soon to be shattered.

In college I had played the defensive middle guard position. The Rough Riders shifted me to the outside linebacker position on the right side. The club expected miracles from me, but I wasn't accustomed to the line-backing position. Besides, Canadian football is a great deal different from the American game. During the first part of the football season, my playing was far from brilliant. I was a disappointment to the club.

I believe that I could have overcome these handicaps and played good football if I hadn't experienced a psychological and spiritual letdown. I forgot the effort that it had cost to play good football during my senior year in college. I was under the illusion that I could play good football without really trying. I didn't give the game everything that I had in practice and preparation.

My play was so poor that the owner of the ball club, with five games still to play in the season, called me in. The owner and one of the coaches asked me to sit out a couple of games and to let them use some other American football player. They took me off the active roster. At that time a Canadian team could have only twelve playing Americans on the ball club. Of the thirty-six active players on the team, only twelve could be Americans; the rest had to be Canadians. There were always several American players waiting in the wings if one of us faltered. American football players usually add quality to a Canadian club. I was told that I would be put back on the active roster later. For two weeks I didn't even suit up for the games.

Mavis and I had not fully adjusted to the severe northern winters in Canada. During the weeks that I did not dress for the games I suffered a terrible case of the flu. Mavis had it just as bad. We were both sick and despondent. For several days we didn't even leave our apartment. One day, while sitting in front of the picture window of our apartment and watching the heavy snowfall, I asked Mavis a question.

"How did I get in this condition? How could I play good football last year and not play it again this year? Why does everything seem to be against us this year?"

We talked about it for a long time, and finally both agreed that I just wasn't giving the game my best. The only solution was to go back and try as hard as I could. Both of us got down on our knees and recommitted our lives to God. We asked His blessing on my efforts in the future.

When the ball club returned from a road trip to Vancouver, I swallowed my pride, went over to the head coach's house, and begged him to let me get back on the active roster. To my surprise he agreed to let me

Vernon was 10, I was 3 when this picture was made outside our home in Bloomburg, Texas. Vernon became a great quarterback at Rice University.

The folks at home still call me "William." (I was 4 years old, and started playing football the next year.)

had my 11th birthday in Corpus Christi, where played Junior High and High School football.

Football has provided a great platform for speaking about the things I've found are best in life for me. Since I was a teenager, I've enjoyed speaking to groups of all kinds.

The lineup of our family: Mindy, 2; Bobby, 6; Billy, 7; Mavis and Bill.

Photo by Ron Kuntz

All of us like the cold Cleveland win —and the kids love the happy hallow at our seasonal home.

play in the three remaining games of the year. My motivation to play had returned. I had recaptured my desire to play with everything that I had. I had asked God to restore my zeal for the game.

The Rough Riders had not had a good year. With three games to go, we were finishing the season in third or fourth place in our division of the League. It was wonderful to get back on the active roster. I was determined to prove to myself, to my Canadian teammates, and to the American players, that I could play. In the first half of the next game I intercepted two passes, made many tackles, and put on a spectacular (if I do say it myself) performance. In the two remaining games of the season I continued to vindicate my renewed commitment. The owners of the ball club were pleased and wanted me to come back to play for them the next season.

When the football season ended in Canada, I returned to the States to take up my theological education. Nobody really thought that I could get all of my seminary work done in the off season. Seminary work ordinarily involves three years of residence work, two semesters each year. The Southwestern Baptist Theological Seminary in Fort Worth, Texas, was willing to let me start and go as far as I could during the off season. I bought a small home in Fort Worth, Texas, for our growing family and started to Southwestern Seminary in late January of 1958 and continued through May. I got a full semester's work in after my first season of pro ball. I continued this for the first six years that I was in pro football. Thus I resolved the dilemma that faced me upon graduation from college. I continued in pro foot-

ball and I continued my preparation for a Christian
vocation. In May of 1963 I finally received my Bachelor
of Divinity Degree from Southwestern Seminary.

After my first year with Canadian football, I experienced real indecision as to whether or not I should go
back to Canada or stay in the States to play with Detroit. The business manager of the Detroit Lions had
worked on me all spring to get me to leave Canada and
come back to Detroit. Never before in the history of
the two leagues had a player jumped from Canada to
America without experiencing great difficulty. When I
had signed with the Canadian League, there had been a
verbal agreement with them that if I wanted to come
back to the States I could do so. To my surprise they
honored this verbal agreement. I was able to jump my
contract without difficulty and to sign up with Detroit
for the 1958 season, my rookie year in American pro
football.

In 1958 when I joined the Detroit Lions I met Watson
Spoelstra, the sports writer. Waddy had come to know
Christ about six months before I came to Detroit. He
came to know the Lord during the crisis of a brain
aneurism his daughter had. With his daughter near
death, he knelt in the chapel of a Catholic Hospital. He
knew that for a long time he had been shunting God off
to one side. Somehow this illness of his daughter was
used of God to bring things into perspective for him.
He was converted that night. He hadn't been inside a
church since he was fifteen years old and at that time he
was in his late forties. I was one of the first Christians
that he talked with after his conversion and it was my
privilege to show him some important things about

Christian growth. He memorized Scripture by putting passages on small cards. He bought several modern translations of the Scripture and we made careful comparisons between them.

While we were in Norman, Oklahoma, playing a preseason game, Waddy and I met Dr. Hallock, pastor of the First Baptist Church of Norman. Dr. Hallock told Waddy,

"Like a great bird, I soar to spiritual heights when I keep both wings in motion. One wing of the Christian life is Bible study and the other is prayer. When I keep both wings flapping, then I soar to God's presence. If I stop using either of these wings I plunge to earth and spiritual destruction."

Waddy took this analogy seriously and studied his Bible and prayed each day. As a result, he grew by leaps and bounds into one of the most mature Christians I know.

Waddy and I became very close friends during the four years that I was with Detroit. We spent time together in prayer and Bible study. However, we had to keep our friendship secret. As a sports writer, he was in a curious and somewhat delicate position. Neither of us wanted it to appear that I was deliberately playing up to a sports writer. This would jeopardize my relationship with my teammates. Waddy was one of the top sports writers in Detroit, but he went out of his way not to be partial to me in his writings in the paper. We sustained each other with our Christian fellowship. Before games I would find out his hotel room number and go there for Bible study and prayer. This was encouraging and strengthening to both of us.

Waddy and I began to bring other Christian players into these meetings and turned them into group meetings. Waddy soon became a correspondent for Christian athletes, and he constantly keeps in touch with us. Most of us in pro sports get at least two letters a month from Waddy in which he encourages us in our Christian lives.

After I had been in Detroit for a couple of years Waddy became a sort of booking agent for me. Every time Detroit played out of town, Waddy would line up a speaking engagement for me on Saturday night before we played the game the next day. He arranged for me to speak for Youth For Christ rallies, before study groups, in homes, and everywhere he could. He did a good job of keeping me busy speaking on the nights before the games. This was a real opportunity to speak for Christ in many different American cities.

I played offensive center most of the 1958 year for Detroit, plus some at defensive end. I played at least half of the game time during this rookie year. Charlie Ane was the first string offensive center, but had to play offensive tackle if someone got hurt. In 1959 I was shifted to defensive end and played most of the game time. In 1960, my best year with the Detroit Lions, I became an established pro defensive end. In 1961 I suffered a minor ankle injury which didn't keep me out of any games, but slowed me down just enough to keep me from doing my very best.

When I was a rookie with Detroit they had two of the greatest quarterbacks in football—Bobby Layne and Tobin Rote. Both were established pro quarterbacks and both were temperamental. As a rookie center I had great difficulty in pleasing them. Both were demanding as to how the ball should be centered to them. Layne was particularly tough on me as a rookie. He made life difficult in many small ways. At every meal he demanded that I stand on a chair, place my hand over my heart, and sing my school song. This was doubly painful for me and for everyone else because I am such a poor singer. He "cussed me out" a number of times because I didn't center the ball to please him. Many of the derogatory things which he said about me were difficult to swallow, but this was part of being a rookie in those days.

In the middle of the year Layne was traded to Pittsburgh and I was moved to defensive end for Detroit. In my new position as defensive end I had to rush the offensive quarterback. I always had my best days when we played Pittsburgh. Since the passer was my old friend Bobby Layne I had a renewed desire to get to the quarterback. We played against Pittsburgh two or three times a year for the next few years. In 1962 we threw Pittsburgh for a total of 90 yards in losses during one game, and I hit the quarterback a number of times. I think Bobby may have gotten the message. I still think of him, though, as a great quarterback and an unforgetable character. I wouldn't have missed knowing him for anything.

In 1962, along with two teammates from Detroit, I was traded to the Cleveland Browns. It was a six man trade—Jim Ninowski, Bill Glass, and Hopalong Cassady from Detroit for Milton Plum, Tommy Watkins, and Dave Lloyd from Cleveland. Waddy phoned to tell me that I was a part of the trade about an hour before I was notified by our head coach, George Wilson. My first reaction to the trade was one of surprise and disappointment. An hour later when George Wilson called to tell me of the trade, I had regained my composure and had decided that this trade was the best thing. Wilson was very apologetic. He said that he hated to trade me and felt that I was one of the better defensive ends in the league. However, Cleveland wouldn't consider making the trade unless I was in it. Cleveland had lost one of their defensive ends, Jim Houston, to the service, and they had to have someone to replace him. I know that Coach Wilson was just trying to be nice to my ruffled feelings, but his words were quite encouraging to me.

When I was traded to Cleveland I began to play better football. I experienced a renewed zest for the game. I recaptured some of my old enthusiasm—something of the great desire for quality football which I had as a senior in college and something of the feeling that God was in my football career. My motivation was strong. God blessed my efforts. The year 1962 was one of the best years I have had in pro football.

Post season games have provided me some satisfying moments. At the end of the 1962 season I was invited to play in the Pro Bowl, the All-Star game of professional football, in Los Angeles. I was privileged to play again in the Pro Bowl game in 1963 and 1964. These bowl games at the end of each season have been memorable ones for me.

In 1963 the quarterback for the opposing team was Bart Starr. Early in the game he faded back to throw a screen pass. I rushed him, jumped as high as I could, and tipped the ball with my fingers. The ball bounced in the air and when it came down, I was waiting with open arms. I grabbed it and ran for our goal line. Starr reacted quickly and attempted to tackle me. I stiff armed him and tried to get him out of the way. I had just shaken him off when another tackle hit me from the back; but I got the ball down to the twenty-five yard line where we were in position for a field goal. My brother, now head coach at Lamar Tech in Beaumont, Texas, has a completely different account of my run for the goal line. He says there was nothing between me and the goal line except green grass, and I was so slow they caught me from behind and tackled me.

Having won the World Championship in January, the Browns were playing against the college All-Stars in Chicago in August of 1965 in the Chicago Tribune All-Star Game. One of the All-Stars whom I was playing against had earned quite a reputation for excellence in college. The Cleveland coaches assured me that he was the finest offensive lineman on the All-Star team. He was powerful and strong, but not as effective in pass blocking as he should have been. Many college linemen aren't good pass blockers because the passing attack isn't as important in college football as it is in pro football. I was able to maneuver around him quite a number of times throughout the game to succeed in getting to the passer. On one play during the game he held me illegally. After the play was over I said,

"A fine football player like you shouldn't have to hold me."

When he came out of the huddle for the next play he apologized, saying that he couldn't seem to stop me except by holding me. About half-way through his statement of apology, the ball was snapped. Evidently

he had forgotten the snap count, but I was watching the
ball even though I was taking in every word of his
apology. I fired across the line of scrimmage, got around
him and threw the quarterback for a loss while the
lineman was still trying to apologize to me. He'll be a
great pro . . . and he'll learn to concentrate on the ball
and make his apologies later.

CHAPTER FIVE

A Distinctive Fellowship of Concern

In the National Football League there are a number of wonderful evangelical Christians from various denominations. After every game I have the opportunity to be with Christians on the opposing team as well as those on my own team. I root for my Christian friends on the opposing team to do well in their play even though I want my team to win the game. We who are Christian football players follow closely the careers of other Christian professionals in various sports. I enjoy a close relationship with Bobby Richardson, Felipe Alou, and others in pro baseball. When Bob Timberlake was a college athlete, I wrote him a letter of encouragement and told him that I wanted to be his friend when he came into pro football. Christian athletes pull for each other and form a close fellowship of concern.

In 1960, Detroit was playing Baltimore. We were winning the game with only a few minutes left to play. With forty seconds left in the game, Johnny Unitas

faded back and threw a long pass to Lenny Moore.
Moore leaped seven yards, caught the ball on the end
of his fingers, and crossed over for a touchdown. That
was the most fantastic catch I have ever seen. The fans
from Baltimore stormed out of the stands and covered
the playing field. The Baltimore fans were in front of,
behind, and all over our bench. They were yelling at the
top of their voices. Some were drunk and many were
obnoxious. One of them stopped in front of one of the
Detroit players, and said,

"Yea! Yea! Yea! We won the game!"

Our player hit the man in the mouth with his helmet,
and knocked him sprawling. I was so mad at Baltimore
and especially the Baltimore fans that I almost felt like
doing the same thing. I was in a sour mood and felt like
venting my anger on the fans who were yelling in my
ears. Finally, the police cleared the field and we continued the game. Baltimore kicked the extra point which
put them five points ahead of us. With thirty-five seconds left in the game, Baltimore kicked off; we got the
ball, and ran it back to about the thirty-five yard line.
We had time for one play. Our quarterback faded back
and threw a pass over the middle to Jim Gibbons, our
end. Baltimore, in guarding the sidelines to keep the
receiver from running out of bounds, left the middle
wide open. Gibbons ran sixty-five yards for a touchdown and we won the game. The final gun sounded
when he was on the twenty-yard line, but the play was
still in effect and we made the touchdown. It was a sad
day for Baltimore. The Baltimore fans, only seconds
before yelling like Comanche Indians, were now completely silent. I saw Don Shinnick, a member of the Balti-

more team and a very fine Christian, coming across the playing field toward me. I assumed that he now felt toward me as I had felt toward Baltimore only seconds before. But to my amazement, he had a smile on his face. His one statement was,

"Thank God."

I said,

"What in the world do you mean by that? How can you be thankful after being beaten?"

And he said,

"Well, you know, like Paul the Apostle, I have found that whatsoever state I am in, therewith to be content."

I knew losing like that hurt him deeply, but his attitude was wonderful. He was gracious and friendly. I was overwhelmed by his genuine Christian attitude in the face of defeat. His Christian maturity was far beyond mine. Only a few minutes before when we were losing, I had been ready to crack someone's head.

When I joined the Cleveland Browns in 1962, I shared with others the wonderful privilege of showing three different players on the team what it meant to be a Christian. Jim Ray Smith, a teammate of theirs, had lived the Christian life before them and they had become vitally interested. It was important that these three young Christians have a proper foundation in the Christian life. We started with a Bible study fellowship group and met every Friday night in a different home. There were six couples that met together—the Shofners, the Smiths, Mavis and I, and the three couples who had just become Christians; and we continued this fellowship group all through the playing season. After supper together we would begin our ·discussion group. We started with prayer. I was the group leader, but I tried not to talk any more than anyone else. Each member of the group discussed a passage of Scripture. For example, we worked through Ephesians, taking one chapter each night. We rewrote the chapter in our own words, averaging eight words per verse. If there were ten verses in a chapter, we had an eighty word total in our summary. When we rewrote the passage in our own words, we were surprised at how well we came to know the passage. The Apostle Paul has some introductions to his letters. In our attempts to rewrite his introduction in the most contemporary English, we'd just say "Hi!" We felt that this was what he was trying to get across in our modern day language. The summaries were all very interesting, and we all received some wonderful help from our work on the Scripture. It was also amazing how much these new Christians grew in Christian understanding after rewriting these passages in their own words. We would start by letting each person read his passage summary and by having a discussion of each summary after it was read. Then we would go back around the group having each person tell what he thought was the key verse, and have a discussion of that. We'd go back around the group for the third time asking each person to tell how this passage blessed him personally. We would conclude the evening by having each person in the group pray a brief prayer. There was probably more genuine Christian growth in this little group than would have ever been possible with another method.

In witnessing to my fellow teammates about Christ, I try to be quite careful to avoid the appearance of being a moral policeman. No player is ever attracted to Chris-

tianity if I put myself in the position of spanking his
fingers. This is something I constantly guard against. I
want my teammates to think of me, first of all, as a
fellow human being. I don't want them to think of me as
the "good guy" on the team. If I have been effective to
any degree in sharing my Christian life it's because my
teammates don't think of me as someone who is there
to censure them—a "holier than thou" type of individual
who is interested in cleaning up the morals of the team.
I tell them that the important thing in their life is that
they come to know Christ as a person. I believe very
strongly that when a person comes to know Christ this
experience is going to have an effect on his moral behavior, but I never want to put the cart before the horse.
I want to introduce my teammate to Christ and then
let Christ show him what is right or wrong in his life.

CHAPTER SIX

Off Season, The Hardest Season

A lot of people ask me what I do when I'm not playing football. Well, for a long time I was in graduate school. But my time is mostly divided now between family, preaching, and staying in condition.

For six consecutive off seasons, I went back to Southwestern Baptist Theological Seminary in Fort Worth, Texas. I continued my theological education for so long that I had more longevity than some of the professors. Some of my closest friends were men on the faculty, since they were there during the entire time that I was a student. I came to know some of the faculty well. They are great scholars and fine Christian gentlemen who are warm in their attitude toward people, and have a profound spiritual life. There I came to understand that outstanding scholarship and a profound Christian faith could be combined in the same person. There were times in my Christian development when I felt that scholarship and Christian warmth didn't go together.

At Southwestern Seminary, I learned the reverse of this. I enjoyed my seminary work immensely. It gave me the opportunity to find satisfying answers to the probing questions of philosophy that had bothered me in undergraduate school. I learned to think in a systematic way concerning the Christian faith. I learned to be a better student. I learned how best to construct the messages that I would be preaching through my years as a Christian minister. Many of my questions about personal growth and spiritual development were answered. I began to build a theological libary of my own.

While at Southwestern Seminary I developed my first interest in owning a bookstore of my own. A close friend, for whom I had a great deal of respect, started a bookstore in Fort Worth that ultimately developed into a book chain. I had a personal interest in the bookstore chain and in the person who headed it. I invested financially in the chain. But my friend suffered a spiritual breakdown which led to an emotional and family breakdown and a financial collapse. The whole company went down the drain and I lost a great deal of money; but more than the loss of the money, I hated to see him go under. He virtually threw his life away, and yet I feel there is still hope for him. This was a disillusioning experience to me; but I think it moved me a step closer to spiritual maturity.

Pro football needs the Christian witness as does any other vocation. It would be a terrible thing if all professional athletics were deserted by Christians. We live in a sports-minded, sports-mad country, and people are interested in what the pro athlete has to say. About fifty million people a week watch the pro football player on television. For Christians to neglect this area of life is to miss a wonderful opportunity. It is important that I witness to my teammates about Christ, but my wider sphere of witness is to the millions of people who are interested in the game.

Because of this, I have preached in every conceivable type of situation during my years in the seminary and during the last eight years in pro football. I have preached in Protestant and Roman Catholic churches. I have spoken at football banquets. I have talked to in-numerable assemblies—in junior high school, high school, and at colleges and universities. I have preached before every type of youth convention. There were 10,000 young people attending a recent Youth For Christ Convention where I spoke. At the Baptist World Alliance Meetings in Miami, Florida, I was privileged to speak briefly to Christians from all over the world. I gave a brief testimony before a national television audience for Billy Graham this year. I mention all of these not to prove that I'm a great preacher, but to show what a wide audience is available to a pro ball player who tries to speak and live for Christ. Other Christian athletes are having these same kinds of experiences.

In addressing young people I try to keep up with the current events. Young people have a language and vocabulary all their own. Their world is not the world of adults. I try to deal with the current problems that teen-agers face. I attempt to give relevant answers to their philosophical and psychological dilemmas. In doing this, I use as much of my football experience as will be meaningful for them. Football is a popular sport among teen-agers. I find that if I can hang a Christian truth on

The people who depict the big pro football lineman as a hulking, non-thinking brute sort of hack me. I take pride in being part of a group of well educated, alert, physically capable men.

Sonny Jurgensen, of the Washington Redskins, probably didn't smile back after we dropped him for a loss on this play.

Photo by the Cleveland Press.

proved to be the turning point of the game happened on this play in the Brown's 42-20 win over the New Giants. I (80) somehow managed to dislodge the ball from halfback Dick James (47) for a New York le and a Brown's score.

Photo by Frank Aleksandrowicz

Jim Brown is the greatest runner in pro footba...

The moments spent backed up against your own goal line are the toughest. This picture, taken when I with the Detroit Lions, catches some of the tense, hard drama of this goal line stand.

Courage is the first virtue of the quarterback. Ed Brown of the Pittsburgh Steelers may not have known I was about to hit him, but he'd have been almost as cool and daring even if he'd known there were two of us about to pounce on him.

Head coach Blanton Collier continually works keep us at peak efficiency. He's a great coach good man.

Photo by Ron K...

a football hook, it tends to stay in their minds. Football illustrations capture their attention, and I can move on from this to a Christian truth.

Week-end meetings seem to be especially effective in reaching young people. After speaking on Friday night, I like to spend all day Saturday talking with high school and college age kids. One good way of meeting them is to have interested teen-agers bring their friends who aren't Christians to a recreation day at the church on Saturday. We set up for ping pong, volleyball, shuffle board, and various other games. I usually spend some time lifting weights with some of the boys. After this physical recreation, I get together with several of the young people at a time, discuss their relationship to Christ, and show them what it really means to be a Christian.

One of the first times we had a session like this was when I spoke at a series of meetings in a church in Ripley, Mississippi. Mavis was there with me. The co-captains of the high school football team were eager to bring some of their friends to the meetings, but when we called on them we found few of them at home. Finally, the boys said to me,

"Why don't you stay at home while we go get them and bring them back to you?"

Those two co-captains gathered their friends into the recreation room of the house where I was staying. I talked with small groups of boys about what it meant to be a Christian. Mavis was upstairs at the same time talking to groups of girls who came. We talked almost all day long for four or five days. Both of us almost lost our voices. High school athletes from several surround-

ing towns came. Many became Christians. I learned there
that personal contact can be as effective as preaching
from a pulpit.

Every year it gets harder for me to be away from my
wife and kids for any length of time. Thus far I've managed to rent a home for us.

We are trying hard to be Christian parents. Because
I'm away so much, Mavis has more to do with training
the children than I do. She reads the Bible and simple
devotional books to them, and then asks them questions
about what she has read. I read to them as often as I can.
There are two books published by Concordia Publish-
ing House which we both like to read from—"Little
Visits With God" and "More Little Visits With God."
All three of our youngsters seem to be at ease when we
talk together about our Christian faith and spiritual life.
Sometimes they put profound questions to us and we
struggle to give them an answer which is honest—but
which they can grasp. It's good spiritual exercise for
Mavis and me . . . tests our own comprehension of truths
we might otherwise mouth glibly.

Once, after Billy had heard me preach about Nico-
demus and the necessity of the New Birth, he called for
his mother sometime after he was supposed to be in bed
asleep. He just couldn't understand what I had been
talking about when I said each of us had to be born
again. Mavis explained it patiently, and simply, as both
of us had tried to do many times before. This time,
though, he grasped the basics so thoroughly that he
readily accepted Christ as his Savior. In fact, he wanted
to wake up Bobby and explain it to him.

In our home and while we're traveling we have thanksgiving sessions. Each of us mentions things which he is thankful for. The children thank the Lord for food, their mother, sometimes their father, their house, for living in a free country, and for their playmates. Once we had some guest passes to a State Fair and one of them was thankful that we didn't have to pay to get in. But other times they show a surprisingly deeper understanding of life when they give thanks for Jesus, for His death on the cross, and for His coming into the world to show us what God is like.

We have found that gripe sessions are almost as essential as thank-you sessions. During these times, we gripe about anything that we dislike about each other, things around home, or almost anything.

This doesn't mean that our home is a democracy. I feel my responsibility keenly, and I'm sure Mavis does. I don't believe it's fair to our kids for me to abdicate as head of the house. We do try to be as creative and helpful as possible when we discipline the kids. Sometimes, when everything else fails, we have to punish them with a spanking. Most of the time though the denial of some privilege is effective. Mindy is just as active and full of energy as the boys are, and having to sit still in a chair for fifteen minutes is pretty rough punishment for any of them.

Our children seem to enjoy having a pro football player for a father. They enjoy traveling. There's a break in routine after the season is over which I'm sure is attractive. It may be that they like to get back to warm Texas and away from the cold Cleveland winter. But sometimes they want me to retire so that they won't have

to go back and forth between Cleveland and Waco each
year.

God has blessed me with a wonderful family. One of
my greatest joys is to share a Christian home with them.
Our children know that their daddy will not always be
a pro football player, but they are already aware that my
vocation as a Christian is a life long commitment. They
know that, along with athletics, God wants me to share
the good news of Christ with other people. It is my
fondest hope that our children will so grow in Christian
understanding and maturity through the years that they
too will sense God's call to make their vocation Christian.

I make an effort to stay in good physical shape during
off season. Playing golf is relaxing and I enjoy it, but it
is not violent enough to keep me in top form. Besides,
golf takes a great deal of time. Handball is the ideal
game. It's tough, hard work. But I can play a game of
handball in about an hour and a half and go right back
to studying or working. There's no time wasted, sitting
around waiting for the foursome ahead to play out of
the way. Isometric contraction is great for off season
conditioning, too. I lift weights just enough to keep
muscle tone and some bulk in my muscles. Running is
very important, in season and out. I do lots of wind
sprints, particularly forty-yard dashes. Every year, on
the first day of training camp, all the players on the
team are tested for speed. I try to keep my speed somewhere around five seconds flat for forty yards.

Part II

CHAPTER SEVEN

Pieces of Glass

JIM BROWN

A sportswriter, in an attempt to needle Jim Brown, asked him during an interview, "Why don't you jump up and run back to the huddle between plays like everybody else? I have noticed that after you are tackled you invariably get up and walk slowly back to the huddle." Jim replied, "Well, I have noticed that they don't record what you do between the plays in the record books. Besides, if I jumped up and ran back to the huddle between plays early in the game I would burn up much of the energy I need for the latter part of the game. Also, if I were injured on one play, I couldn't run back to the huddle and the opposing team would know that I was hurt. When I go back to the huddle slowly the opposing team never knows when I am hurt or when I am tired." Jim Brown may walk slowly back to the huddle, but he is still the greatest runner in football.

LAZY ATHLETES?

The difference in my little boy's behavior on Monday morning and on Saturday morning teaches us the meaning of motivation. On Monday morning, he rises from bed with a thousand excuses as to why he shouldn't go to school that day. On Saturday morning, he bounds from bed at the unearthly hour of four o'clock because we're going fishing. He yells at me, "Get up! Let's go! What are you waiting for?" I have never met any lazy athletes—just unmotivated ones. Properly motivated, there is almost nothing that an athlete can't do. An athlete with tremendous potential but poor motivation soon finds himself dropped from the lineup.

DON'T WORRY ABOUT GETTING HURT

In speaking at football banquets, boys often ask me if I have ever been hurt playing football. I reply that I've been very blessed in that I have never received an injury serious enough to cause me to miss a game throughout my three years of junior high school, three years of high school, four years of college, and eight years of professional football. I have never suffered a serious football injury. Most good football players never even think about getting hurt. They forget that injury is a possibility. Their main concern is to carry through their assignment on the field. The good football player knows that if he constantly thinks about getting hurt his mental state will be one of growing anxiety. He knows that he won't play as hard as he should and, therefore, will make himself more vulnerable to injury. I feel that parents are unduly concerned about their children suffering injury in football. Actually, more young people are injured each year in automobile accidents than are hurt on the football field. Athletics are good for young people. Parents would do well to be more concerned about those unhealthy avenues open to young people that drag them down physically, mentally, and spiritually. Athletics are a healthy alternative to fill the empty void created by the innumerable unwholesome activities open to young people in our society.

IS THIS GAME FIXED?

Football is unlike wrestling. Some joshingly say that wrestling is the safest sport for old men. In football the player gives each play everything that he's got. Y. A. Tittle says that he has played in only one game which he thought was fixed. He was playing with the San Francisco Forty-Niners in an exhibition game against New York. Tittle says that when the New York tacklers rushed in to hit him they lowered him to the ground gently. When they did actually knock him down, they quickly helped him to his feet with the greatest show of concern. The New York tacklers were constantly asking him, "Are you all right? Are you hurt?"

He was unaware that just before the game started he had been traded to New York and that this had been announced in the New York dressing room. Every New York player on the field knew that Tittle would soon be their new quarterback. Not until the game was over did he learn that he had been traded to New York and that the game was not fixed.

WHO SAYS LIFE HAS NO MEANING?

The history of philosophy speaks of many wise men

who have pointed us in the direction of the meaning of
our existence. Jean Paul Sartre, a leader of French cafe
society and a proponent of atheistic existentialism, has
told us that existence is meaningless. Many people have
taken him seriously, accepted his gloomy philosophy,
and suffered the consequences. A popular form of his
thought pervades many American campuses, inspires
the nihilistic literature in our bookstores, and shapes the
realistically gloomy movies of Hollywood and Europe.
How can we expect our young people to lead anything
other than a hollow existence when they are constantly
surrounded by this pessimistic propaganda? If our young
people are saturated with the thought that life has no
exit, we need not expect them to recognize a Christian
ideal when confronted with one. Life has no meaning
only for those who have no cause to give themselves to.

THREE AND OUT
"Three and out" yells the defensive lineman as he
thunders onto the field. This is his battle cry. Most
defensive linemen don't play on fourth down because
there is a punt receiving team that comes in for them.
By "three and out" the lineman means that he will play
for three downs, hold the offensive team of the opponent
for the three downs and force them to punt. Then he
goes out for a rest. "Three and out" has a special meaning for a defensive lineman.

SECRET DISCIPLESHIP
"Coach Brown," I said, "I have just been traded from
the Detroit Lions to your team, the Cleveland Browns.
The Detroit Lions wear beautiful blue jerseys. The
Cleveland Browns wear a drab brown jersey which I

don't like. I want to continue to wear the beautiful blue jersey of the Detroit Lions. I'll play for your team, but don't make me wear your jersey."

Of course, I never said anything like this to Paul Brown. No player would ever be so foolish as to argue with the coach about wearing his uniform. If you play for a team, you wear its uniform. Yet there are too many Christians who refuse to wear the proper uniform. There is no secret discipleship of Jesus Christ. Every Christian should wear the marks of the Christian faith openly and proudly.

CONTROL THE BLOCKER

As a defensive end I must control and destroy the block before I can make the tackle. I use three different techniques in controlling the block. In the "forearm shiver" I deliver a blow with my shoulder and snap my forearm up. I extend my arms and grab the blocker's jersey to control the blocker. In the "double forearm shiver destroy" I make a head-on charge delivering a blow with both forearms, extend both arms, and control the blockers. The third technique that I use is the "hand shiver", used on the pass rush when the offensive linemen have dropped back. I strike a blow with my extended arms and grab the jersey to control the blocker.

PROFESSOR, WATCH THAT WAISTLINE

When I attended theological seminary during six consecutive off seasons, I became close friends with many of the professors. I once chided Dr. Jack McGorman, chairman of the New Testament department, because for years he had prepared himself mentally and spiritually, but had never done anything to develop himself physically. He agreed that this was true. He said, "The heaviest thing I have picked up in the last fifteen years is a pencil." I told him that he should be ashamed of himself. I assured him that he was going to die young and that he probably wouldn't have any zest while he was alive. He took my good-natured remarks seriously and began to "work out" with us. He dropped a lot of weight, took five or six inches off his waist, firmed up his chest and shoulders, and before long was in good shape. This was very impressive to his fellow professors and some of them began to follow his routine. Many people, when around an athlete, try to give the impression that they are fine physical specimens. I often chuckle silently at the fellow who sucks in his normally pooching stomach to make me believe that he once had great athletic potential.

THE DEFENSIVE UNIT THAT WENT TO SLEEP

The twelve teammates had worked for Him for three years. During the championship play-off game one teammate proved to be a traitor. Eleven remained for this final contest. Satan's defenses were momentarily checked when eight of them threw up a good front line protection. Peter, James and John, responsible for furnishing the close protection, went to sleep. In the Garden of Gethsemane Jesus fought off Satan's advances alone. Singlehandedly He won the victory that brought all men into a new relationship with God.

ON WHICH TEAM DOES THE OFFICIAL PLAY

Officials help the game run smoothly. Without them it would be chaos. I have played in games in which I felt that the officials interfered too much with the course of the game, and in other games in which I felt they didn't officiate closely enough. I feel that the perfect game is one in which the officials call it close, but not overly close. I don't like to hear unnecessary criticism of officials; they do their best. I have never been in a game in which I felt that there was dishonest officiating. At times, however, I feel that officials have made mistakes. In a recent game the offensive tackle was holding me a great deal when I tried to rush the passer. This is illegal, and I complained to an official (not an NFL official). He didn't respond and didn't call holding on the tackle. I was so unhappy with him that at one point I said, "You know, your guy is holding me again." He said, "What do you mean, your guy? I'm not coaching that team." I said, "Oh, pardon me. I thought you were."

SHAVING POINTS

Coaches advise their players that if they're ever approached on shaving points they should simply say, "I'll have to think it over," and then report it to the management who will report it immediately to the League. Coaches are cautioned by the League to watch carefully those fans who become closely associated with clubs, particularly those who might be seeking information for betting purposes. A new Federal statute states that any telephonic communications across the state line for gambling purposes is a violation.

WATCH YOUR LANGUAGE

The League office says that both players and coaches must conduct themselves in a manner above reproach to avoid giving the fans and press a reason to criticize. Officials are advised that they're not to tolerate abusive language by players and coaches. To avoid penalties as well as embarrassment, all coaches are urged to stay off the playing field during the game.

A CASUAL TACKLE?

When I play defensive end for the Cleveland Browns, I get down on the line of scrimmage in a stance of complete intensity. Every muscle in my body is tightened to fire across the defensive line. Just before the ball snaps my body is one of complete concentration. The first movement that I see on the other side of the line sets me off like a gigantic spring into my opponent. I hit him as hard as I can. I grab him and throw him to the inside. Then I whip to the outside and try to rush the passer with everything I've got. Can you imagine a Christian lining up on the defensive line of the Christian life casually? I see a lot of casual Christians. What if I, as a defensive end, lined up on the defensive line in a football game like some casual Christians try to serve Jesus Christ? A defensive end that lined up like that would get knocked on his casual can. And a Christian who tries to serve Jesus Christ casually will be highly ineffective. The New English Bible, New Testament says, "But because you are lukewarm, neither hot nor cold, I will spit you out of my mouth." (Revelation 3) A lukewarm Christian nauseates God.

DEFENSIVE CHARGE

Like other defensive ends I have a standard procedure when I charge. I drive off the rear foot over the forward foot, extend my body, and deliver a "forearm shiver" to neutralize the blocker. I come to balance as I control the blocker. If my roll off is with a lead step, the blow is delivered as I take the first or second step according to the block. My basic defensive principle is to attack the man that attacks me, keeping my position in my lane of responsibility. I react to the offensive blocker as I roll off, whether it is from the inside or the outside of my lane.

ALCOHOLIC BEVERAGES

A League rule prohibits alcoholic beverages in the dressing room of the players, and coaches stress that this rule must be observed. The club does not tolerate any abusive language or filthy talk at any time or place.

GOOD LOSERS USUALLY LOSE

Sometimes in speaking engagements people have whispered in my ear, "Talk to 'em about being a good loser." I usually say, "Really, I'd like to, but I don't have any material on the subject. Everything is bad about being a loser. There's nothing good about it." They reply, "Oh, you know what we mean." "No," I retort, "I don't know what you mean. There's nothing good about it; it's all bad."

If you get beat, after the game is over you ought to congratulate the winner. Shake his hand and tell him what a great game he played; pat him on the back. Yes, practice good sportsmanship. But, when you get in the dressing room and no one is looking, back off about ten yards and run and ram your head into the locker because you hate to lose so badly. Don't ever be a good loser. Be a bad loser. Good losers usually lose.

THE TV TRIANGLE TO WATCH

Many football fans have asked me how they might better watch a professional game on television. They say that they usually end up watching only the progress of the ball. They don't see the play develop because they watch only the line blocking. Therefore they don't understand what type of play is being run. They follow the line of least resistance and watch the ball only. I always suggest that they watch the triangle of the center, both guards, and the quarterback. If the television viewer watches this triangle he can tell from the instant that the ball is snapped what the play will be. Ninety-five percent of the time the two guards will tell the fans which way the play will go. For example, if both guards pull and go to the right, then it is going to be an end run to the right. If one guard pulls to his inside across the center, then it will probably be a trap play or a play up the middle. If both guards fire across the line it will obviously be a play up the middle. If both guards drop back into a pass protection blocking stance, the fan will quickly know that a pass play is developing. If the football fan will keep this triangle in mind, he can follow the play from its very beginning, watch it develop, keep his eye on the ball, see the blocking pattern, and observe the entire play with awareness.

DON'T ACCUSE MY FATHER OF
PLAYING FOOTBALL

My son Bobby found a hole in the adjoining yard where our neighbor intended to plant a tree. The tree was a week late in arriving, so Bobby had a wonderful place to play for several days. Our neighbor was upset about Bobby playing in the hole because he was afraid Bobby would hurt himself. For several afternoons he ran Bobby out of the hole. One afternoon he drove into the driveway and saw Bobby in the hole again. He jumped out of his car, slammed the door, ran over to where Bobby was playing, and said, "Bobby, I thought I told you to stay out of that hole." Bobby stood to his full three-year-old size in the middle of the hole, placed his hands on his hips, and demanded loudly, "Do you know who my Daddy is?" My neighbor didn't want to give Bobby the satisfaction of knowing that he knew me, so he said, "No, I don't know who he is. Who is he?" My neighbor thought that Bobby would say that his Daddy was a big football player and that he would knock his block off. To his surprise, however, Bobby said, "He's a Christian." My neighbor was speechless, but he had to reply in some way so that Bobby wouldn't think that this was anything so different or out of the ordinary. He said, "Then *you* be a good little Christian and get out of that hole." Bobby said, "All right, I will." So he got out and trotted back home.

YOU CAN'T WIN FOR LOSING

Johnny Unitas of the Baltimore Colts is one of the greatest quarterbacks who ever lived; yet he wasn't quite good enough in the championship game of 1964 when we beat them 27-0. Johnny was quite conscious of this for the entire week after that game. Dozens of people asked him, "You have the greatest offense in the country and yet the Browns held you to no points. What happened?" In a few days Johnny was so tired of hearing the question, "What happened?" that he never wanted to hear the name Cleveland Browns or Jim Brown again. A few days later Johnny was traveling to the Pro Bowl game on the West Coast for a post season game. As he got on the airplane he said to himself, "Now I can read a magazine, take a nap, and I won't have to think about our defeat until I get to California." As he settled into his seat he found that the passengers were going to watch a movie. He thought, "This is just what I need to relax me." When the movie came on, it was "Rio Conchos" starring Jim Brown of the Cleveland Browns.

DON'T LET THE RAIN COME DOWN

Not long ago I was listening to some music on my car radio. One of the songs went like this: "There was a crooked man who had a crooked house. He had a crooked cat. He had a crooked style and he had a crooked smile." I chuckled to myself as my mind flashed back to this nursery rhyme of childhood. But then the chorus went on, "Ah ha, ah ho, don't let the rain come down. Don't let the rain come down. My roof's got a hole in it and I might drown". This was not the happy ending of a youthful nursery rhyme. This guy was in bad shape. He was about to drown. There was no way out for him. He was trapped; but this song realistically exemplified much of the thinking of con-

temporary young people. In stark contrast to the chorus
of this song, Jesus Christ has come to say that there is
meaning, purpose, and direction for life. Granted that
life presents its many traps for young people—God has
provided a way out for them.

DRESS WHILE TRAVELING

A memorandum from Pete Rozelle in the office of the
Commissioner indicates squad discipline about dress.
The contract signed by each player states that he will
wear a coat and tie while traveling and appearing in
public places. It is up to the coaches to see that this rule
is enforced. Our coaches know that the people in the
National Football League are constantly in the public
eye, and must avoid any action, statement, or form of
dress which might be called to the attention of the public and openly criticized.

GET TO KNOW YOUR COACH

Johnny Unitas is one of the greatest quarterbacks in
pro football. You may sit in front of Johnny Unitas'
locker for the rest of your life, but that won't make
you like Johnny Unitas. You may wear his uniform,
but you still won't be the passer he is. If you could
somehow boil his talent down and pour it into you, then
and only then could you be like him. You may sit in
church the rest of your life, but that in itself won't make
you one bit more Christ-like. You must have Christ in
you. And though you could never actually have Johnny
Unitas' talent in you, you can have Christ in you. No
less than this will do. If you are to be very effective in
the Christian life, you must know the Great Coach and

be able to take instructions from Him. The Christian life summarized in two sentences is: First, that you come to know Him. Second, that you come to know Him better.

CROUCHED AND BALANCE POSITION
This is a fundamental position from which a defensive lineman can control blockers and make his tackles. When in this position we carry our arms dangling in front of our knees so that we can prevent blockers from getting to our legs and body.

TO ERR IS HUMAN
Blanton Collier, our head coach, is under the influence of the "zero defects" program of the United States Defense Department. As a result he has tried to tell us on the team that people make errors in proportion to the amount of importance they attach to their particular job. Most workmen make about five per cent errors on their job; yet they will not allow five per cent errors in other areas of their lives. They won't allow this percentage of errors in their pay check. They always go to the house that they call home; they never go to a strange house 5% of the time. Blanton Collier will not allow us to excuse ourselves for making mistakes. To play a football game without error is a high and possibly unattainable goal. Nevertheless, it is a goal that our coach is determined that we strive for.

ASTRODOME
The Astrodome Stadium in Houston is great because it takes the weather factor out of an athletic contest.

The most capable team in any athletic contest is going to win unless the weather becomes a factor during a game. Bad weather usually helps the weaker team. The perfect weather conditions in the Astrodome enables the better of two teams to play consistently good ball. No football player enjoys playing in excessively hot weather. We played in Dallas against the Dallas Cowboys in 110 degrees weather. I didn't think I was going to live through the game. When it was over I had to almost crawl off the field. I lost 20 pounds in that one afternoon. Freezing weather presents another handicap to the professional football player. When the ground is hard and frozen we have to wear tennis shoes. During rainy weather, the field becomes slushy and muddy and makes movement difficult. The Astrodome Stadium removes the chance in the weather factor.

THE EXTRA YARD

Self-control is an essential part of every athletic contest, but it is especially so in football. At top speed a back runs down the sideline with the ball. He weighs one hundred and eighty pounds in full dress uniform. A three hundred pound tackle closes in on him. The only way that he can possibly avoid the bruising, bone-jarring collision with the huge tackle is to step out of bounds. It has always been difficult for me to understand what keeps that little back from jumping out of bounds, dashing up into the stands, and sitting with the girls. Yet he always plunges head-on into the tackler and makes an extra yard or two for his team. Self-control is the secret that keeps him on the playing field.

THE MOMENT OF TRUTH

The Tuesday morning after the Sunday game is the moment of truth for professional football players. We look at the films of the previous Sunday's game. No matter how well we think we executed a maneuver, no matter how much we congratulate ourselves on our brilliant playing, when we look at the films we never did quite as well as we thought. The films don't lie. There it is in black and white, blown up to bigger than life size on the huge screen for the whole team and the coaches to see. The coaches might mention briefly some good play that you made, but they never fail to point out in detail your every mistake. In one game I had missed a tackle. When we came to that place in the film, the coach said, "Just a minute. Stop the film. Run it back." The film was stopped and the coach said, "Now run it back through again. Let's see if Bill makes the tackle this time." Since it was the same film, I naturally missed the tackle again. The coach said, "Let's run it back again. Maybe he'll make the tackle this time." Again I missed the tackle, but you can bet that I tried not to miss a tackle in the next game.

GOD FORGIVE ME

When I was a junior at Baylor I was asked to visit a six year old boy in the hospital. The little boy, Bobby, was completely paralyzed from polio. Bobby loved the game of football and his friends thought that a visit from a football player might encourage him. When I went to the hospital to see Bobby I took him a chin strap that we had used the week before when we played against the University of Texas. I talked with Bobby about football and all the sports. I talked to him about hunting, fishing, and swimming. Yet I found it very difficult to talk with him because I had been told that he would never walk again. I didn't have very much in the way of encouragement to give him and I felt like a bull in a china closet. Suddenly Bobby's mother said, "Look, Bill, isn't that wonderful?" Bobby's face was glowing with obvious pride. I would gladly have complimented him but I couldn't see anything to justify his and his mother's pride. Then Bobby's mother pointed to his hand. The index finger of his right hand was moving just a little. He was overjoyed at the ability to move one finger. When I left the hospital room that day I looked all the way down my healthy body to my size fourteen shoes and prayed this prayer, "O, God, forgive me. Forgive me for being so ungrateful for the strong healthy body that you have given me. Help me to use my good health in a better way for you."

AMERICAN LEAGUE

This League is very helpful to the players in it as well as to the players in the National Football League. The American League gives us leverage in salary discussions; and it permits more athletes to play because it can soon field as many professional football players as the National League. Many people have asked me if there will ever be a playoff game between the American League and the National League. I think that there will ultimately be such a playoff, but I don't see it any time in the near future.

PASS RUSH

If the defensive line gives the opposing quarterback

time to throw the ball, he will murder them. The defensive lineman must rush the passer to keep him from throwing the ball. He always hopes to tackle the passer. If he can't tackle the passer, he hopes to block the pass. If he can't block the pass, he hopes to put enough pressure on the quarterback so that he cannot find his receiver. If the quarterback can't find his receiver he may throw a wild pass which always presents the possibility of an interception. With these things in mind, the defensive lineman exerts his every effort to put pressure on the quarterback.

RACE AND FOOTBALL

I was in the home of a wealthy thirty-five year old man. After hearing me speak in his city, he had been eager for me to join him for a meal at his home. He was seemingly impressed with what I had to say about the whole field of athletics. I had been informed that he had keen prejudices and that I would be wise not to display my convictions about integration. I had just settled myself for a chat with him in his home when he asked, "Bill, how is it playing with those Niggers?" I said, "Would you try to imagine something with me?" He said, "Sure." I said, "Imagine that from childhood you loved athletics. As you grew older, you found yourself more athletically gifted than other kids your age. You were faster, bigger, stronger, and tougher. You were a good student in school. When you went to college you were the best football player that had ever attended that school. When you entered pro football, you were offered a fantastic contract. You had great physical ability and you could perform well under the pressures of the pro game. Tremendous business opportunities opened up before you. But in spite of all these advantages you have one problem over which you have absolutely no control. That is—you're black. If you can imagine this you can imagine how the colored player feels when he is treated like a second class citizen." We must forget color and treat everyone alike.

PULL YOUR SOCKS UP

During the game, coaches are responsible for maintaining the principles of neatness in dress for players. On the playing field the athletes try to keep their shirt tails tucked in and their socks pulled up.

KNOW YOUR OPPONENT

One year I was playing in the Pro Bowl, which is the all-star game of professional football. Playing next to me on the defensive line at the tackle position was a guy named Lipscomb—"Big Daddy Lipscomb." Well, "Big Daddy Lipscomb" had always played on an opposing team. When I was with Detroit, he was with Baltimore; and when I was traded to Cleveland, he was traded to Pittsburgh. I had never thought of Lipscomb as anything but an opponent. He had always been on an enemy team. In this Pro Bowl game we were both on the Eastern division team. I looked over to my left, and there was "Big Daddy Lipscomb." What if I had forgotten and had decided, "Uh-oh, he's my opponent," and had turned on him and rammed into him instead of my real opponent across the line? Not only would I have gotten hurt, but it would have left a tremendous gap on our side of the line. Our opponents could have made a great gain through our side of the line. But I had it clear in my mind—"He's my teammate, and I must treat him like a teammate. There is my opponent over there on the other side of the line, and I've got to treat him like an opponent." Many Christians have confused their teammates with their opponents. They think the enemy is a sister church, or a different denomination, or what's worse, a person within their own group. The enemy is not a person at all, he is a spirit called Satan. Anybody who is a Christian is a teammate.

GOOD NIGHT, SLEEP TIGHT

Coaches are always on the watch to see that the players get a proper amount of rest before the game. Coaches disconnect the player's hotel room phones at curfew time. Coaches want the players to be in contact with the fans but they don't want the fans disturbing the sleep of the players after curfew hours.

48-32-232

These are the measurements of Jim Brown. He has a forty-eight inch chest, a thirty-two inch waist, and he weighs two hundred and thirty-two pounds. Jim is one of the best built football players in the history of the game and one of its fastest runners. His excellent physique explains in part why he is such a fantastic runner and pass receiver. He is one of the finest athletes in pro football.

CELL GROUP

A cell group is a small unit. We know this term most recently from Communist cell groups. The idea of the cell group has degenerated since New Testament days. Christians of the first century had no church buildings of colonial or gothic architecture. They met in small groups in the homes of fellow Christians. They had no Bible, no hired preacher, no monolithic structure. They met in small intimate groups to share their pains and their joys. The twentieth century church is seeing a return to the idea of the cell group among its members. Small groups of Christians are meeting inside the church building and outside of it to discuss their faith in Christ. They feel the necessity of growing spiritually through participation. Many of our churches today need to grow out of the lecture room mentality. This denies the individual Christian the privilege of participation because the classroom atmosphere produces spectators rather than participants. What Christian wants to share his intimate problems as well as his victories with five hundred passive people in an open assembly? The fellowship of the small group makes for healthy Christians.

A REMINDER TO LAST YEAR'S CHAMPIONS

What you think and feel about the game of football is of ultimate significance in being a winner. Authorities say that winners seldom repeat, but it has been done and can be done again. To be last year's champions is a just cause of pride. But this year you are just one of fourteen teams fighting for the championship. You must select your goal and dedicate yourself to achieving it for this year and forget about last year's victories. If you want to win again, know your job thoroughly, do it correctly every time, and be aggressive in your play.

BILLY GRAHAM

In January of 1965 I had the privilege of meeting Governor Frank Clement of the State of Tennessee. The governor, while we were discussing his friendship with Billy Graham, told me of a golf game he had played with Billy in Nashville. During the game, he and Billy grew hungry and decided that they would get a snack. When the governor suggested that they go to a hamburger place about five blocks down the street, Billy wanted to know why they couldn't eat there on the course. The governor said they could but the only place available was a bar. Billy said he didn't mind eating in the bar because he had no intention of getting drunk. While ordering the sandwiches in the bar, Billy leaned across the table to the governor and asked if they could exchange seats. Billy was facing the bar and the governor was facing the wall. After exchanging seats the governor asked the reason for the seat swapping. Billy said, "I feel that the guy at the bar who's drinking the scotch and soda would enjoy it a great deal more while looking at a politician than he would while looking at a preacher." The governor asked Billy why he wasn't obviously and more openly critical of drinking. Billy answered, "Billy Graham is not God. I don't pretend to be a moral policeman; I'm a spokesman who introduces people to Christ while Christ is the one who will help people to properly evaluate their behavior."

CALISTHENICS

Our coaches tell us to enter into the spirit of exercises at all times. The way we take our exercise routine tends to indicate our attitude toward the game.

THE MEANING OF A KISS

Not only did the New Testament Christians love their Lord enough to die for Him, but they were willing to die for each other. Part of the magnetism of the first century Christianity was the comradeship among Christians. Even the non-Christians said of the Christians, "Behold, how they love one another." They really cared for each other. This amazed the non-Christian world. An unusual practice grew up among these early Christians. It was called the "Holy Kiss." I was baffled about the "Holy Kiss" when I read about it in the New Testament. "What is the Holy Kiss?" Finally I decided to do some research on the subject. I discovered to my amazement that the "Holy Kiss" grew out of the persecution that came in the first century. These Christians never knew when there would be some big Roman soldier waiting around the next corner to drag them off to jail or to some horrible death. And so, every time they came back together after they had been separated for several days, they would greet one another with a "Holy Kiss." "Oh, I'm so glad to see you. I'm so glad you haven't met death or torture." Thus they would greet one another with a kiss. It was a spontaneous show of affection that grew out of the terrible insecurity of their world. By the third century there had come so many polluting streams into the life of Christianity that the church legislated against the "Holy Kiss." Thereafter the men kissed only the men and the women kissed only the women. The "Holy Kiss" died a natural death in one generation and has never been heard of since in Christianity. I'm not suggesting that we bring back the "Holy Kiss," but I am suggesting that we bring back to our Christian lives something of the same spirit, something of the same harmony, something of the same teamwork, that the "Holy Kiss" was a sign of.

THREE-POINT STANCE

The fundamental stance for a defensive end on the line of scrimmage is a three-point position. If possible the outside hand is down. The feet are placed firmly on the ground. Weight is fairly evenly distributed on all three points. The back is parallel with the ground. The inside hand is under the shoulder.

WORK WITH YOUR TEAMMATES

Our 1964 World Championship season took the effort of every one of our 40 players, our whole coaching staff, and the front office. Jim Brown was important to the championship, and so was Frank Ryan. But what were they without great blockers, good pass receivers, and a fine defense? Don't forget the fine effort of our kicking teams, made up in the main of so-called second string players. They played a major part in winning at least three games for us. What's a great team without good coaches? What are great coaches without a good front office? And what is all of this without a helpful and co-operative owner? Every athlete knows the importance of team work. A team cannot depend entirely on one star player. A team can't be made up of prima donnas. There must be many men working together on a professional football team. It takes all of us; we're no stronger than our weakest players.

So it is in the Christian life. Everyone must work together. If there is no teamwork within our churches we will be ineffective in reaching the world for Christ. We cannot expect to be effective if we operate as isolated islands. We must operate together as a mighty marching army. Guerilla warfare does little good. Teamwork is just as important in the Christian life as in football. You contribute most to the cause of Christ through cooperating. Only as you are a vital part of the Christian team can you grow to spiritual maturity.

STAY IN SHAPE

Our coaches insist that we keep in proper physical condition, ready to play at all times. This is the responsibility of each player. The coach cannot do it for him. Our physical condition indicates the degree of our dedication to the game. We must keep our weight down, run to keep our legs strong, and hit in every practice to maintain body toughness.

WHAT PARENTS DON'T KNOW
WILL HURT THEM

Many parents aren't concerned with the live issues among teen-agers. They are not aware of what's going on in the lives of their own children. Too often parents are concerned with the tame issues, such as holding hands, when the live issue among some young people is whether or not they will sleep together. Young people today are farther along in their understanding of life than they were at a comparable age ten years ago. They are reaping the results of the bold immorality found in contemporary movies, books, dramas, and TV programs. Their parents were never confronted with these secular philosophies when they were kids. Strangely enough, I have found that those most concerned about immorality among teen-agers are the high school athletic coaches. A number of high school coaches have told me that their biggest problem in coaching the young men in their school is to get their minds off illicit sex long enough to get them interested in football.

THE GUTLESS WONDER

The big six-footer stands trembling before the twelve-year-old boy. The man is urged by God's Holy Spirit to talk to the little boy about the boy's need for Christ. The big man could play defensive tackle on anyone's team; but when confronted with the little boy, he gets a yellow stripe down his back a mile wide. He can't find the courage to share his Christian faith. He says to God, "I'll do anything you ask. I'll be a deacon in the church. I'll read my Bible. I'll pray. I'll give money, but please don't ask me to talk to this little boy about his need for Christ." Everything is within his power, but he is afraid to give away the most meaningful thing in any man's life. And when confronted with a man his own age he's really a "gutless wonder."

FINES

Our coaches realize that they cannot buy the attitude of the player, but they insist on a series of fines to help the player understand the seriousness of what the coaches are trying to do. It is $500 for going out after curfew any night the curfew is in effect; $500 for the loss of the play book; $100 for any infraction, such as disorderly conduct, drinking, and/or any action detrimental to the welfare of the team; $100 for missing the plane or bus when traveling, plus paying your own expenses to the game with the earliest possible transportation facility. There is a $50 fine for every fifteen minutes you are late after curfew; $25 for being late for any practice or meeting; $50 for unexcused missing of meals at any time when provided by the club; $100 for failure to get permission from Coach Collier not to return with the team following a game on the road; $50 for failure to practice in a sincere and satisfactory manner; $25 for extreme horseplay when traveling, in rooms or locker room, risking possible injury and creating dissension on the team; and $100 for each day of practice missed. All fine money is donated to charity. The charity is determined by the players at the end of the season.

PURSUIT

As a defensive right end my main desire is to make the tackle. First I must work through the blocker and destroy the block. I throw off the blocker and come in for the tackle. I slide or spin to the hole, but spinning is only a last resort. I drive through my defensive point and look for the run or the draw play. If the play is a pass play I put on a burst of speed and power as I rush the passer hard. I drive through the blockers protecting the passer and move in on the passer for the tackle.

THE WORST THING THAT CAN BE
SAID ABOUT A PLAYER

Blanton Collier, our head coach, always tells us that the worst thing that can be said about any player is that he is uncoachable. This simply means that he won't pay attention to what his coach tells him. A player must be able to take coaching and listen to instruction. And when the going gets tough, he must be even more careful about taking the signals of the coach. Most players know their coach so well they don't even have to talk to him during the game because they know what he wants them to do.

THE PRIVATE EYE

When Paul Brown was head coach of the Cleveland Browns, he always suspected the opposition of spying on his team and getting all of the team plays and secrets. When the Browns were in training at their camp at Bowling Green, Paul Brown spotted a suspicious looking car parked on the highway about 150 yards away. It was raining heavily and the team was sloshing through its workout. Coach Brown sent Morrie Kono, the equipment manager, to run the car off because he thought it was spying on the workout. Morrie ran through the rain and mud to the car and found a salesman, with his suits hanging in the back of the car, sound asleep on the front seat. Morrie returned to the coach and said, "It's just a salesman and he's sound asleep. He's probably been driving all night and just stopped for a nap. I didn't want to wake him." Coach Brown said, "You never know. Run him off." Morrie returned to the car once again, woke the man, and told him that he couldn't park there. The yawning, sleepy-eyed salesman slowly drove away to find another parking place.

THE WHITES OF THEIR EYES

Being a defensive end, it is my job to rush the passer.

First, I drive my blocker toward the passer, looking at
the passer's eyes as I move in. The passer's eyes and
movements will usually tell me what he is going to do.
I mustn't let the passer out of his pocket. Secondly, as I
drive toward the passer, I make sure that a draw play
is not developing. The draw is a play designed to look
like a pass but is actually a delayed running play up the
middle. Third, when the passer begins to throw in my
direction, I get my hands up to block the pass and force
the passer to throw over my hands. Fourth, if I reach
the passer before he can throw I tackle him high around
the arms and try to force him to fumble.

WE WERE BETTER THAN HE THOUGHT

Blanton Collier says that he always dreads looking at
the movies of a game because we usually look worse
than we thought we were. Movies always reveal those
mistakes and hidden weaknesses that you were unaware
of during the game. In preparing for the 1964 championship game, we had worked long and hard. When
Coach Collier looked at the movies of this game, he was
pleasantly surprised. He said that each player had learned
and carried out the details of his assignment during the
game. We were better than he thought we would be.
After looking at the movies, Collier told us that if we
are to win the championship again, we must remember
how we got there in 1964 and do it again. He pointed
out two problems we will have. First, we can grow
complacent about being the 1964 champions and forget
how we came to be the champions. Second, our opponents will be better than ever and they'll be shooting
at us because we're now on top.

GET YOUR STORY STRAIGHT

Frank Ryan, my roommate with the Browns, was talking with the quarterback for the Washington Redskins before a practice session at the 1965 Pro Bowl game. A sports writer overheard Ryan say in jest, "If Namath is worth $400,000, I am worth a million dollars." The next day this statement was headlines all over the country. Frank felt terrible about it because it made him sound arrogant. Yet there was nothing he could do except complain to the sports writer. Never say anything to the press that you're not willing to see in print.

IS PRO FOOTBALL DIRTY?

Pro football is rough, tough, spirited, exciting, and has lots of pressures, but I don't feel that it's dirty. It's cleaner than college football.

HE'S NO BALL PLAYER

When Dick Modzelewski ("Mo") was playing for the New York Giants, he and his teammates were entering the stadium at Canton, Ohio for an exhibition game. Delbert Shofner, their great receiver, was stopped by the gate attendant and told that only football players were allowed to get in without a ticket. Delbert turned to Dick and said " 'Mo', tell them that I'm a player." "Mo" said, "He's no ball player. He's just a skinny kid trying to get into the game free." All the other Giant players that followed agreed with "Mo" that Delbert was not on their team. The gate attendant firmly refused to let Delbert in the stadium until a coach finally came along who would vouch for him.

PLEASE DON'T ARREST ME, OFFICER

The New York Giants were working out at Fordham University during the 1960 presidential election campaign. Republican candidate Richard Nixon was speaking in the gymnasium at Fordham University. Dick Modzelewski, at that time playing with the Giants, was in the gymnasium listening to Mr. Nixon. In the middle of Mr. Nixon's speech, "Mo" and some of his teammates had to leave for a practice session. As they walked away from the gymnasium two FBI agents approached "Mo" and told him that they wanted to ask him a few questions. "Mo" had forgotten that he was still wearing the Russian olympic cap with the red star on the front which he had found in the dressing room. "Mo" turned to his teammate Sam Huff, famed linebacker, and said, "Sam, tell these men that I play with the Giants." Sam said, "I don't know this guy. He has been hanging around here for two or three days trying to act like one of the New York Giants football players." Only when one of the coaches assured the FBI men that "Mo" really did play for the Giants was "Mo" released.

ARE YOU STILL USING THAT GREASY KID STUFF?

In 1963 the Cleveland Browns had beat the New York Giants badly in the first game. After this victory Dick Schafrath remarked that the New York players were highly overrated. Dick said that he couldn't see why the New York players got to make all the commercials on radio and television and were constantly called upon for endorsements of products. He felt that the New York players didn't deserve all their publicity and that other players in the League should get some attention. In the second season game between New York and Cleveland, New York was beating us badly. Dick Lynch, defensive back for the Giants, said to Schafrath late in the game, "I'm going to do a hair grooming commercial tomorrow. I would like for you to come along and play the "greasy kid" part."

I'M GLAD OTTO GRAHAM WAS WRONG

At the beginning of the 1964 season, Otto Graham said that the Cleveland Browns would never win the championship by depending upon Jim Brown. He indicated that Jim Brown was a good runner, but that he wouldn't block. Blanton Collier, our head coach, immediately came to Jim's defense and said, "You don't use a great race horse as a plow horse." But he went on to say that Jim had always done an adequate job for us in blocking. This exchange of opinions became a nationally publicized incident. Everyone on our team came to the defense of Jim Brown's blocking. After we became the 1964 champions, Otto Graham said that the reason he voiced this opinion at the beginning of the season was to needle Jim Brown into a better job of blocking. Whether this was the case or not, I'm glad that Otto was wrong in his first opinion.

THE BOSS CHIMP IS NO CHUMP

Many people today claim that moral standards are relative, yet even among animals the leader scorns relativity. A famous trainer of chimpanzees was asked how he put his troops through their complex acts with such precise control. He said, "First I stand back and watch a new group for a while to see who is going to be boss. Once that is settled I have little difficulty. The boss chimp, once I get him on my side, keeps the rest of them in line." Even the boss chimp is not willing to settle for an easygoing attitude which says that everything is relative.

THE QUIET BEFORE THE STORM

Dick Modzelewski was asked why Jim Brown, his teammate, gets up so slowly after being tackled and calmly walks back to the huddle. "Mo" said, "It's just the quiet before the storm."

A SMALL BOY HELPS THE CAUSE

Every Sunday morning before the game several of us get together for Bible study. The format is simple and informal—a devotional thought, discussion, and audible prayer by those who wish to do so. We are pleased to find that many of the fellows are eager to join us. Sam Bender, a Christian businessman from Toledo, Ohio, and one of my best friends, was invited to bring the devotional thought one Sunday morning to our group. We were surprised but pleased to find that he had brought his eleven year old son with him. The thought that morning centered around the "adequate Christ." It was reassuring for us to hear that we could do all things through Christ, who is our strength. In two hours we would be facing the New York Giants in a very important football game. During our time of prayer, Sam's little sixty-five pound boy was seated between a 245 pound defensive end and a 255 pound tackle. When the boy's opportunity came to participate, he didn't let it

pass by, but talked intimately with his Lord. He asked
that the Lord would help us play our best. He prayed
that we would remember to thank Him in victory, and
for the opportunity to live for Him as professional athletes, and to remember that any earthly glory we might
receive should be returned to God. After the group
broke up Paul Wiggin, our defensive left end said, "I
thought I was about to get out of grade school in the
Christian life. But after hearing his prayer I feel that I
am back in the first grade."

FAIR WEATHER FANS

Bill Wade, quarterback for the Chicago Bears, led
his team to the 1963 National Football League World
Championship. But in 1964 Chicago had many bad
breaks and a great many misfortunes. They ended up
near the bottom in the League standing, and as a result
Wade became an unpopular quarterback among the
Chicago fans. After almost every game, his wife left
the stadium in tears because of the rudeness of the fans.
When Chicago was playing Detroit, Alex Karras broke
through the blockers and hit Bill with a crushing blow,
breaking one rib and knocking him unconscious. When
Bill came to, the first thing he heard was the cheering
of the crowd. Bill said that it wasn't so bad when they
booed because he wasn't doing well, but that it was
almost too much to take when the fans cheered when he
got hurt.

ANYTHING TO PLEASE THE COACH

When Paul Brown was head coach of the Cleveland
Browns, he was with the team at Chicago's Soldier Field

for an All-Star game. Some of the players complained to Coach Brown that the dressing room was excessively hot. They said that the steam heaters were about to suffocate them. Coach Brown sent Morrie Kono, the equipment manager, to check with the maintenance officials to see if the heat could be turned off. When Morrie returned a perspiring and nervous Paul Brown asked if the heaters had been turned off. Morrie replied that he was working on it. Coach Brown said that it was not enough just to work on it, he wanted the heaters off now. Morrie went back to the frustrated stadium officials and told them that the coach was very upset. The officials explained that the heaters hadn't worked in that dressing room for twenty years. So Morrie asked one of the maintenance men to get a hammer and beat on the pipes to make the coach think that the heaters were being fixed and turned off. The reluctant maintenance man agreed to do this only after Morrie had given him a $5 bill. When Morrie returned to the dressing room, he found Coach Brown all smiles because he could tell from the banging noise that the heaters were being repaired.

ALBERT EINSTEIN ON RELATIVITY

Dr. Einstein was asked what would happen to human morals if intelligent life was found on other planets. Einstein replied that the universe is fully consistent; it is a unity. The same physical laws that regulate the movements of our planet control the most distant stars. Likewise, the moral laws that govern us hold sway in the furthest regions of the universe. Einstein evidently didn't go for the theory of relativity in the realm of moral behavior.

PAUL BROWN

When Paul Brown left the club at the owner's insistence, many people were critical of him. I liked him because he traded for me and got me on a great club, because he was always very fair with me, and because he seemed to need a friend. Some of my teammates said that I had played under him for only one year, and that he had mellowed a lot before I got to know him. He still deserved the Hall of Fame.

THE POOR BOY'S LEG IS BROKEN

Abe Gibron, offensive guard for Cleveland during the 50's, was All-Pro a number of times and one of the great guards in the League. During one unusually violent play he heard his leg "pop" and knew that it was broken. The trainer, the team doctor, and the equipment men rushed onto the field to aid him. Abe, with his lips set in pain, groaned that he knew it was broken because he heard it snap. They wanted to rush Abe off the field, but he said, "My mother is in the stands and she will be worried sick if she sees me being carried off on a stretcher." The team doctor decided to cut the leg of Abe's game pants to see how bad the break was. When he slit the pants he discovered the source of Abe's "pop"; the elastic tape, wrapped tightly around Abe's leg, had snapped, making the loud sound which Abe thought was his leg being broken.

LOU GROZA

A San Francisco paper said, "He's the man with the big stomach and the strong legs." I think of him as a fine person and a sure shot for the Hall of Fame.

GET IN THE GAME

Sam was a great athlete, but he had one problem. After some thought he decided he'd make a deal with his coach. His coach was a reasonable man; he thought something could be worked out. Sam picked a good time and made an appointment with his coach. "Coach, I want to make a deal with you. I like everything about football except one thing, and you can help me at that point. It's not much that I ask." The coach interrupted, "What's your deal?" Sam said, "Well, coach, I want to really work. I want to be the best blocker, tackler, runner, passer, and kicker that you ever coached." The excited coach replied, "Yes, and you could be just that." "But, I have one minor request, coach." "Whatever you say, Sam." "Coach, all I ask is that you don't make me play in the games."

You say no player would be that crazy. But are you any better when you won't serve God where it really counts? You may be a spectator Christian, sitting on the sidelines cheering others. You need to get off the bench and into the thick of the real battle.

THE TURNING POINT

In almost every game there is a turning point when it becomes obvious that one team is going to win. There may be several minutes yet to play, and there may yet be a genuine struggle, but it becomes obvious to both teams and to every spectator that one team has the victory. Almost two thousand years ago, in the death and resurrection of Jesus Christ, God won a victory over the forces of evil in the world. This turning point in world history is not evident to everyone (many do not even know that history required a turning point), but the Christian is fully persuaded that God won a decisive victory over the evil forces that were crippling man and keeping him from spiritual maturity. No matter how bleak things become the victory has already been assured.

DO MY FANS STILL LOVE ME?

Don Paul, defensive back for the Cleveland Browns, was knocked out during a game against the Chicago Cardinals in the late 50's. Leo Murphy, our trainer, rushed on the field to see how badly Don was hurt. As Leo worked over Don he called loudly several times, "Can you hear me?" As Don slowly came to Leo called again, "Don, can you hear me? Are you all right?" Don mumbled, "I'm all right, but how's the crowd taking it?"

HOW CAN A PRO FOOTBALL PLAYER
BE A CHRISTIAN?

I am asked this question many times, and I'm often tempted to treat it lightly and reply facetiously, "Just like in any other profession." But I have been asked the question so often that I feel that there must be a misunderstanding about what it means to be a professional athlete as well as what it means to be a Christian. A stereotyped image of a football player is that he is a big, dumb, rough, insensitive hulk who doesn't know what the world is like off the playing field. Many spectators don't seem to realize that many times the pro football player is a well educated, sensitive, warm human being. Football players are good citizens and family men. Sometimes the picture drawn of the Christian is even more distorted. Christianity does not teach a withdrawal from life, but an infiltration of it; the Christian is not a policeman for everyone's conduct, but rather an ambassador of the good news about Christ. A Christian athlete has a double motivation: first, he wants to give to his team the very best that he can; second, he wants to be as good an athlete as he can because his ability on the playing field gives him the respect off the field that is necessary to win the confidence of people for Christ.

WHO'S YELLOW?

Two boys were talking in the Athletic Dorm at Baylor University. One played end for us and the other half back. The half back said, "I wish you'd face your need for God in your life. Accept His Son and become a Christian. You know it's right for you. Why don't you do it?" The end said, "I know you're right. I need God. I do intend to become a Christian some day, but not tonight." As he walked through the door leaving the room, he said, "Maybe later." The half back said, "What's-a-matter, no guts?" That's all he said. The end froze in the door, turned, and walked back into the room. He grabbed his teammate by the hand, shook it firmly, and said, "You hit the nail right on the head—that's just my problem. But tonight if He'll have me, I want Him." He became a Christian.

Sometimes we feel that we had rather do anything than introduce a friend to Christ. Yet we know that we are doing our friend the greatest service possible. He is potentially our brother in Christ.

Part III

LET'S PLAY THE GAME

ter six springs of graduate work, I
eived my Bachelor of Divinity degree
m Southwestern Baptist Seminary, Fort
orth, Texas in 1963.

Mavis and I went to Hawaii in 1965 for
a large youth convention. We met some
wonderful people.

I must admit that even in the spring
d summer my mind often goes back to the
tball field, to the joy of "hand to hand"
nbat, the Browns, and Blanton Collier.

FRONT ROW: (Left to Right), Leo Murphy (Trainer), Blanton Collier (Head Coach), Fritz Heisler (Assistant Coach), 27 Walter Roberts, 24 Bobby Franklin, 23 Larry Benz, 35 Galen Fiss, 49 Walter Beach, 30 Bernie Parrish, 36 Charley Scales, Nick Skorich (Assistant Coach), Morrie Kono (Equipment Manager), Ed Ulinski (Assistant Coach).

SECOND ROW: Dub Jones (Assistant Coach), 26 Dave Raimey, 11 Jim Ninowski, 42 Paul Warfield, 50 Vince Costello, 74 Dick Modzelewski, 67 Sidney Williams, 87 Tom Hutchinson, 20 Ross Fichtner, 38 Stan Sczurek, 44 Leroy Kelly, Howard Brinker (Assistant Coach).

THIRD ROW: 48 Ernie Green, 52 Mike Lucci, 85 Clifton McNeil, 13 Frank Ryan, 70 John Brown, 60 John Wooten, 77 Dick Schafrath, 82 Jim Houston, 66 Gene Hickerson, 22 Lowell Caylor, 32 Jim Brown, 62 Dale Memmelaar.

FOURTH ROW: 76 Lou Groza, 86 Gary Collins, 79 Bob Gain, 69 Jim Kanicki, 73 Monte Clark, 80 Bill Glass, 78 Frank Parker, 83 John Brewer, 75 Roger Shoals, 56 John Morrow, 84 Paul Wiggin.

Our 1964 World Championship Team is a definite example of what hard work and team work can accomplish. They're a great bunch of guys.

CHAPTER EIGHT

Play Fair

In 1963 we were playing the St. Louis Cardinals in St. Louis. We had them backed up on their own five yard line. Charlie Johnson, their quarterback, faded back to throw a pass. I was rushing in from the defensive right. Paul Wiggin, our other defensive end, was rushing from the defensive left. The official was standing about five yards behind Charlie Johnson deep in the end zone. Wiggin weighs about 250. I weigh about 260. We had Charlie sandwiched in between us. We were both running at him at top speed. He was poised to throw the ball. Wiggin was still a little distance away, but I was just getting ready to clobber Charlie from the back. Charlie didn't hear me as I closed in on him. It was one of those things that linemen dream about—getting to hit the passer in the back as he's stretched out before he releases the ball. I could almost hear the thunderous applause I would get for throwing Charlie for a long loss in his end zone. But it was too much for the official watching these two big brutes ready to hit the helpless, scrawny little quarterback. At the last second, the official yelled,

"Watch out!"

Charlie ducked. And when he ducked, Wiggin and I hit head on at top speed. Both of us melted to the ground. Charlie ran free and gained about ten yards. When I came to, the first thing that I remember was seeing the official peering down at me. I couldn't speak above a whisper, so I reached up and pulled him down a little closer so that he could hear me. I said,

"You know, you really shouldn't have done that."

And he said, "Aw, Bill, I'm sorry."

And he apologized both to me and Wiggin, and to our entire coaching staff. That's the first and last time that I've ever had an official apologize to me for anything.

Both fans and players give officials a hard time, but officials are very important to the success of any game. A game without rules and officials would be no game at all; it would simply be chaos. The purpose of the official is to help the game run smoothly and to see that everyone abides by the rules as nearly as possible.

Football is like life—not everyone plays fair. As a defensive end rushing the passer, nothing makes me madder than an offensive tackle who holds. In offensive football, holding is illegal. Any defensive end who has a sense of fair play is infuriated at being held. The player's sense of what's right and wrong, what's fair and unfair, is important. The thing that causes fights in athletic games is one player's feeling that another player has violated the rules of fair play.

I have found that I must play fair with myself, with others, and with God. This is the only way to win in life. I chose to play fair with God when I got on the team of His Son, Jesus Christ. You may say,

"Boy, is that different—a pro football player and yet an outspoken Christian."

I make no apology for being a Christian. I have found that playing fair in life means facing up to God and His claims on me.

"When did all this begin with you? When did you first choose to play on this team, Bill?"

Well, it all started with me when I was about sixteen. I came face to face with one whom I could not sidestep. He said to me,

"I am the way, the truth, and the life. No man cometh unto the Father except by me."

I knew then that the game was already lost if I didn't meet this challenge from God.

"But, Bill, you make it sound so easy."

I can assure you that this head-on encounter with God shook me to my toes. It's like playing defensive end for the Cleveland Browns. Occasionally, when I charge across the defensive line, something odd happens; that is, no one hits me. Usually when I charge across that defensive line either a tackle, an end, or a back hits me. When I charge and no one hits me, I know that something is wrong. It's like the calm before the storm. As I look up I see a 260 pound guard plunging toward me. His teeth are gritted and he wags his head from side to side as he charges. I always have the sensation of being stalled on a railroad track at midnight. The guard's white teeth remind me of a train's headlights sweeping back and forth. I'm stock still in the middle of the defensive hole. The guard is only a yard away, and I know he doesn't intend to do me any good. I know he intends to run over me and, if he can, knock me flat out of that hole. And if I did the thing I really wanted to, I'd sidestep that guy to the outside.

If I'm perfectly honest with you, I don't really want to face all that power head on. But if I sidestep to the outside, he bumps me out a little further, and the back cuts to the inside and they make a lot of yards. On the other hand, I could sidestep him to the inside. But if I do, he'll cut me in and the back will cut to the outside and again they'll make a lot of yards. So the only thing that I can do is that most painful, that most bone-shaking kind of thing; that is, face the big guard head on. Now, that's not comfortable. But if you're going to stop a trap play—that's the only way you can possibly do it. You hope to offset him and stop the play right in the middle of the line. The trap play is an awfully tough play to stop. But there is only one way to do it, and that's to face it head on, right in the middle.

I was just sixteen years old when I faced one whom I could not sidestep. When He said to me, "I am the way, the truth, and the life; No man comes to the Father except by me," He was saying, "I am the only way to God." I wanted to sidestep Him. I didn't want to face Him head on. I wanted to sidestep Him to the outside and say,

"I'm not so bad. I go to church pretty often."

Or perhaps I could sidestep Him to the inside and say,

"I'll turn over a new leaf. I'll change my way of living."

But I came to see that my moral goodness and my attendance at church were only attempts to by-pass the rules of fair play with God. All of these things were simply sidestepping and I feared jumping off into my own destruction. So I had to face Jesus Christ squarely and say to Him one of two things:

"Sir, you are the biggest liar who ever lived," or

"Sir, you are the Son of God and the only possible way to get to God; therefore, I will fall down before you and worship you as my Lord. I will crown you king in my life. Your way shall be my way. Your cause shall be my cause. I will serve you all the days of my life."

I began to play fair with God when I accepted His Son as the Lord of my life. Then it was that God put meaning and purpose into my life. I had experienced the popular philosophy which says that life has no meaning. Jesus Christ came to say the opposite of this. He says there is great meaning, there is great purpose in life. God rescued my life from meaninglessness by giving me a task.

God has chosen to limit Himself to the use of people like you and me to carry out His purposes in the world. And if you play fair with Him then you will realize that He is depending on you to carry His good news to all men. I don't know why it is that God has chosen to do it this way. If it had been me, I might have discarded the whole rotten mess and said,

"I am through with man."

But God loved us so much that He chose to use us to accomplish His purposes. By playing fair with God I became His ambassador.

God loves all people through us, His messengers. God

wants you as His representative throughout all the earth
to tell them of Him and of his love. And if you do not
let Him use you in accomplishing His great plan then
you are cheating God. By not playing fair with God,
you are sinning against the greatest love the world has
ever known. For you see, God loved us so much that
He sent His son down to the field of combat to live
among sweaty, dirty men, to die on a sin-cursed cross,
and to be resurrected from the dead. If we refuse to be
on His team then we're not playing fair with Him and
His great love. We are turning our backs on God's love,
mercy, grace, and forgiveness.

I discovered that when I played fair with God I also
played fair with myself. When I wasn't on His team I
was committing spiritual suicide. If a man kills himself
then you say,

"This man must be crazy to commit suicide."

But he's not half so foolish as you if you say "no" to
Jesus Christ. You're slowly committing spiritual suicide.
You aren't playing fair with yourself.

"But, Bill," you ask, "how am I cheating myself if I
don't respond to Jesus Christ as the Lord of my life?"

First, you are cheating your best potential self because
you and I were created by God in such a way that we
operate best when dedicated to Him and His purposes.
Many people today are going to psychiatrists with emotional problems. The reason for their emotional breakdown is that they have never found anything worth
giving themselves to. Every person needs a cause bigger
than himself to be emotionally healthy. If you find a
cause and give yourself to it, you won't be so self-cen-
tered, so introverted, so concerned with your own little

world. You will, rather, be more concerned with the
outside world and its needs. Christ teaches that we find
ourselves by losing ourselves. You say,

"But how can this be? It sounds so contradictory."

You must grasp what He's teaching you. He's saying
when you lose yourself in service to Him and others,
you find what it is to really live. So lose yourself and
you'll discover what real happiness and emotional maturity mean.

Secondly, if you cheat God you are cheating yourself
by being out of step with the universe. But look at the
positive side of this assertion. When you begin to pull
Christ's way, you are pulling in the same direction as the
Creator of the universe. When you choose to play on
the team of the Lord, then you are choosing to play on
the same team with God. You can feel Him pulling be-
neath the weight of the same cross that you are pulling.
That's no small potatoes! That's big business in anybody's book! Everything else fades into insignificance
when compared to His cause. Yet all of life becomes
shot through with meaning when you're in harmony
with God and yourself.

In the third place, if you don't play fair with God you
cheat yourself out of your future. The Bible says that if
you are rightly related to Jesus Christ and get on His
team, then you become eternal. When all the cheers die
away, when all the star players are forgotten, when all
the stadiums crumble with old age, when the earth itself
is as useless as a forgotten moth-eaten lettersweater—
then you shall have just started to live. Jesus Christ
claims, and I believe, that because I know Him in my
heart I am eternal. Under God your life will take on a

quality that will last forever. God will never let your
relationship with Him be broken in this life or the next.
Jesus told Martha,

"I am the resurrection, and the life: He that believeth
in me, though he were dead, yet shall he live. And whosoever liveth and believeth in me shall never die." (John
11:25-26).

You need to play on His team to be fair with yourself,
to be in harmony with God's creation, and to enjoy
God forever. You need Him more than you need your
next breath. He is life. To have Him is to have life.

Not only do you need to play fair with God and fair
with yourself, but you need to play fair with your fellowman. His is the only team that you can be on and
play fair with others. When I was traded from the Detroit Lions to the Cleveland Browns, I was impressed by
the influence of two guys on the Browns' team. They
were Jim Ray Smith, five times All-Pro guard, and Jim
Shofner, one of the best defensive backs in the League.
They had for years been key players for the Browns and
were also very fine and consistent Christians. They
weren't obnoxious with their Christianity, but they
were consistently for His great cause. Well, within the
first month that I was with the Browns three different
players came to talk to me. All three had similar ap-
proaches.

"Jim Ray and 'Shof' have been telling us about Christianity—now we want you to tell us more."

All three were converted to Christ, and their con-
versions came largely as a result of these two guys who
played fair by sharing their faith. But the story doesn't
end there. Jim Ray was traded to Dallas and his room-

mate there was another guard, Dale Memmelaar. Jim
Ray again influenced his roommate toward Christ. Well,
Memmelaar was traded to us a few months later, and
some of the Christians on our team were the human
instruments used to harvest the crop that Jim Ray
planted.

There are a growing number of National Football
League players who are accepting the frightening
responsibility of their influence. This is the only way
you can really play fair with others. The Christian cause
is the only cause you can stand for and play fair with
yourself, your fellowman, and with God.

You may ask, "Why can't I play fair with others even
if I'm not a Christian?"

You can't because you can never share with your
fellowmen that which you don't have. When you are a
Christian you can experience God's love, emotional maturity, purpose in life, and a wonderful future. If you
can have these, you can share them with others. If you
cheat God you get none of them, and thus you cheat
your fellowman because you cannot pass them on to
him. To a Christian every man is potentially a brother
with whom he can share the good news about God's
love.

Everything to gain by playing fair with God; everything to lose by cheating! I found that it took every
ounce of courage I had to face up to my need for God.
And to witness of the new life in Christ demands renewed courage on my part every day.

There is a tradition of a second century Christian
named Polycarp. He was told that he must die for his
faith in Christ.

"If you don't recant, we'll burn you at the stake."

For three weeks he practiced for being burned at the stake by lowering his hands down into the flame of a candle placed before him on the table in his cell. He would hold his hand in the flame as long as he could, and when he could endure the agony no longer, he would say,

"O God, give me the strength not to recant under the pain of the flames."

We athletes train by studying, running, and scrimmaging. He trained by holding his hand in the flame.

Finally they hustled him out into the Roman arena. They tied him to the stake and piled dry wood all about him. The crowd came by the thousands into the Roman arena shouting gleefully for his blood. As the Roman guard stood nearby with the torch held high in the air, the Roman emperor shouted,

"Polycarp, renounce your Christ and you live!"

Polycarp shouted back,

"Emperor, accept my Christ or you die!"

The torch went down. The dry kindling wood began to burn. The flames leaped up all around Polycarp. He went into eternity singing praises to his God. He did not recant. But don't waste one second's sympathy on Polycarp. Rather, feel sorry for the spineless individual who never really comes to stand for anything; that person who never has the courage to face his need for God and never turns to accept Christ as Savior. That's the person for whom you should feel sorry because he refuses to play fair with himself, his fellowman, and with his God. He loses because he cheats.

CHAPTER NINE

Keep Your Helmet On

Just before my senior year in college I went to the Fellowship of Christian Athletes retreat at Estes Park, Colorado. Christian athletes were there from all over the United States. The one who impressed me most was Donn Moomaw, two-time All American from U.C.L.A. Donn and I quickly became good friends. Before I left I asked Donn,

"Is there any word of advice that you could give a young athlete who is anxious to do his best in football?"

He said, "Yes, Bill, the minute you leave the clubhouse, put your helmet on and don't take it off until you come back in. Do this both for practice and for games."

"But, Donn," I said, "when my helmet gets hot and sticky, I like to take it off and let the wind cool my head. I like to scratch my head when the helmet makes it itch. Especially in practice when the going isn't tough and there is no hard contact, why not take my helmet off?"

111

He said,

"Well, when you take your helmet off you're telling yourself and everyone else on your team that what you are doing isn't really very important. When you take your helmet off you indicate to everyone that you are letting up. So from the minute you leave the clubhouse, put your helmet on and don't take it off until you come back in. This keeps you on your toes; you are always at your best. You let your teammates know that every part of practice is important by keeping your helmet on."

A player with his helmet on is a player on his toes.

Don scored a point for football, but even more of a point for the Christian life. It's very important for every Christian to keep his helmet on. First, a Christian on his toes grabs every chance for service. We can stumble past many opportunities without this precaution. Over there is someone who is having serious problems in his home; you could be of help to him. Over there is a friend who is constantly in difficulty; you could be of service to her. When a Christian slacks up in any part of the game he becomes insensitive to the needs of others.

Second, when a Christian keeps his helmet on he doesn't run the risk of getting a concussion. When the Christian plays a lackadaisical game he may be seriously injured. Carelessness could split his head. To be on our toes is to be fully helmeted against the hard knocks that a Christian may expect from every side of the playing field. To get a concussion is to be out of the game.

I can sympathize with a Christian who responds to this bit of advice by asking,

"How can I be on my toes to grab opportunities for

the Lord when I live in an arena of cut-throat competition? Shouldn't I just try to keep from getting my block knocked off rather than try to influence others for Christ? If I speak to him of Christ, won't he take this as a sign of weakness on my part and use it to gain an advantage for himself?"

Well, I would agree with you that we live in a highly competitive world. Even children are being pushed into fights for grades and social status. But a Christian would never stoop to the kind of success that comes from stepping over the corpses of those clubbed on the way up. The Christian wants to play the game fairly. But in the second place, a Christian never shies away from competition. He is never passive in his attitude.

I face the problem of aggressive competition on the football field. It even gets violent at times. In fact, I feel that I'm obligated to play the game with everything I've got. Football is a contact sport. If I don't hit the guy who's playing across from me as hard as I can, he certainly won't respect me. One way to build respect for what you say concerning your faith is to play the game with everything you've got.

The pro game is amazingly clean. Probably one of the reasons it is so clean is because we play everybody in our division twice. You realize that you will have to play this team again, and if you play dirty in the first game, then you know you've got to play them in another game. Also there is a complete film exchange. If a player were to play dirty in one game, then three teams would see him play that way the following week. The movies are sent to three opposing teams after every game. So there is self-policing among the players.

I remember one day we were playing against Baltimore, and I was playing against Jim Parker. For two or three years I had had all kinds of problems trying to get past Parker, the offensive tackle, to rush the quarterback, Johnny Unitas. I had always tried to hand-fight Jim Parker without much success. Jim weighs about 280 pounds. It was thought by most of us who play defensive end that the best way to get around him was to outmaneuver him by hand-fighting him. But no one had been very successful in doing this. So I felt that maybe the best way to beat him would be to try something altogether different. I decided to get down on the line of scrimmage and fire across as hard as I could just as the ball was snapped. I intended to hit him with everything that I had, grab him and pull him to the inside, and then pull out around him. If I did this I would get past him in time to hit Unitas before he threw the ball. Well, this worked amazingly well in the first game. By the end of the game he was really mad at me. I had gotten by him many times and hit Unitas for several losses. On the next to the last play of the game, I fired into him again, pulled around, and was just about past him when he wound up and hit me with his big left fist right in the stomach. It knocked all the wind out of me. Jim is a boxer in the off season and sometimes he forgets he's not a boxer during the season. The only thing that kept me from falling flat on my face was his body. I draped my arms across his shoulders and looked him squarely in the eye. I could tell immediately that he was sorry that he did it, and sure enough he said,

"Bill, really I didn't mean to; I just lost my temper."

He was very apologetic. And I said,

"I'm really glad you feel that way, Jim, because if you felt differently I couldn't do a thing about it. I've had it."

Life is as competitive as football, but most of the time there are no rules or officials. A Christian should play hard. He should be an expert in his vocation. But he should be fair and honest, because he has a built-in official in his own conscience. You need to keep your helmet on—to grab every opportunity to witness to your non-Christian competitor, to be the best you can be in your profession in order to gain his respect, and to guard against a selfish attitude as you compete with him.

A second reader may say,

"But, Bill, I feel that a few of my fellow Christians are constantly watching to see if I make a mistake. I'm trying to follow God's leadership to more effectively witness for Him. How can I restrict my life the way they say I should if that is going to keep me from grasping the opportunity to be a witness for Christ? How should I respond to my critics?"

I would agree with you that there is nothing more discouraging than getting a concussion from your own teammates. You need to keep your helmet on to guard against a certain interpretation of the Christian life. This requires special sensitivity. Some would require you to be such a negativist that you would find yourself totally separated from the world. This would isolate you from the very ones you want to reach. I had to wrestle with this problem myself over the question of playing Sunday football.

In the Old Testament we see the people trying to find God by keeping rules. The height of this law ob-

servance was reached in Jesus' day by the Pharisees.
They had a never ending list of ridiculous rules to keep
to be right with God. This is known as legalism. Legalism is the idea that you get right with God by doing or
by not doing things. Both Jesus and Paul were fighting
this type of religion all the time.

When people from a Jewish background wanted to
bring into Christianity all the rules of legalism, Paul
charged them with being pseudo or phony Christians.
Paul said that those fake Christians "Wormed their way
into our meeting to spy on the liberty we enjoy in
Christ Jesus, and then attempted to tie us up with rules
and regulations." (Galatians 2:3-4, Phillips Translation)
Paul insisted that the keeping of rules cannot even in the
remotest way improve one's relationship to Christ.

"A man is justified not by performing what the law
commands, but by faith in Jesus Christ. Consequently, I
refuse to stultify the grace of God by reverting to the
law. For if righteousness were profitable under the law
then Christ died for nothing!" (Galatians 2:16 and 21,
Phillips Translation)

Paul says that no Christian could be so idiotic as to
think that a man begins his spiritual life in the Spirit and
then completes it by reverting to outward observances.
We have modern Pharisees, for example, who think
they're good Christians in proportion to the number of
times they go to church per week. A three service Christian is therefore more dedicated than a two service
Christian. They put the emphasis on the outward observances rather than heart relationship to God.

Dale Memmelar and Monte Clark called me into
Monte's room one night when I was walking down the

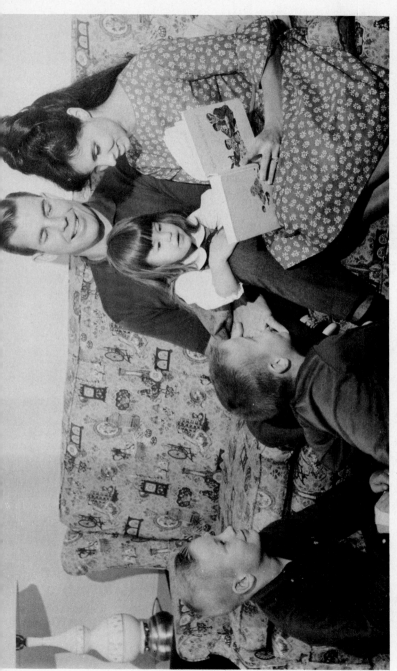

Home is the greatest—and I'm blessed with a wonderful wife and family. I think it's important for a father to participate in family devotions.

Several of the Brown's defensive players take a much needed rest while waiting for the offense to score.

There must be an easier way make a living.

Photo by Tony Tom

Anyone who doubts the roughness of the game in 1965 has never tried to get to quarterback Dick Shiner, of the Washington Redskins. These guys play for keeps.

Photo by Frank Aleksandrowicz

hall during our training camp at Hiram College, Hiram,
Ohio. We were living on the second floor of Centennial
Hall. The coaches had just released us from a night
meeting. I went in and sat on a bed across from Dale
and Monte. Dale was disturbed. He said,

"Some wonderful people that I respect very much
think I am all wrong for playing football on Sunday."

I said, "Well, Dale, I made my decision to play pro
ball on the basis of the great platform that it gave me
from which to influence people. People are interested in
what the pro has to say. They may not listen to the
pastor, but they would listen to a football player. Fur-
thermore, I just couldn't believe that God was willing
for all pro sports to go without a witness just because of
Sunday game days."

Dale interrupted, "I see your point, but what about
the 'Honor the Sabbath Day' commandment?"

I replied, "Raymond Berry was converted after he'd
been in pro football for several years. He telephoned me
one night and we must have talked an hour long distance about this very problem. The day before a kid
had asked him why he played football on Sunday since
he was now a Christian. I tried to tell Raymond how
God had led me."

Opening my New Testament, I began to show Dale
some of the passages I had shared with Raymond Berry.

After reading the Bible and fully discussing the problem, Dale Memmelar was satisfied. But Dale came to
Christ only after we were able to get these legalistic
ideas out of his mind. After we removed the obstacles
of "rule keeping" we were able to show him the meaning of a right relationship to Christ.

I believe that God has led me to play pro football. There are many times when it would be easier not to play. It's tough to drag my wife and three children away from our home in Waco for five months every year. As I grow older it becomes more difficult to get back in shape for the next season. I lift weights, do isometric exercises, play handball, and run 40-yard dashes almost daily throughout the off season in order to be in shape to play. It's no picnic on the field at times either. But I believe that if I were to quit playing pro football now I would be deserting the calling of God. I don't believe God would bless in my play on the field and in my Christian service were it against His will. Jesus asked the question,

"Is it wrong for me to do good on the Sabbath day?" (Luke 6:9)

I believe that Christian athletes have an opportunity to do a great deal of good by playing Sunday football.

I can't answer every question that you can ask about how to face your legalistic critics. But the principle involved in my experience as a Christian athlete may hold true for your particular situation. Dr. E. S. James, editor of the Texas *Baptist Standard* (May 19, 1965) answered a reader about this very problem.

"Most Christians believe Sunday is a day for worship, but they are not agreed on what the people of God may or may not do when they are not at the church. Some hold that every moment of the day should be devoted exclusively to the service of Christ, and others regard it as a day for rest and relaxation from the usual vocations as well as a day for worship. To the latter group it is all right to use the afternoon for entertainment of different kinds, but others regard that as a sin. My own opinion is that if we are going to condemn the baseball and football players whose contracts call for Sunday games, then we ought to condemn all who watch them on television. If we do that, then let us condemn the Sunday afternoon golfers, automobile drivers, and everybody else who does anything on Sunday except attend church services. Perhaps that would even include those who read the morning papers, stroll around the block or go out to eat. Since the New Testament does not give explicit instructions about how to observe the Lord's Day, perhaps it is a matter for every Christian to answer for himself in the light of what he believes God wants him to do."

The Christian, athlete or otherwise, wouldn't be far wrong by following the suggestion of Paul,

"Don't let anyone worry you by criticizing what you eat or drink, or what holy days you ought to observe, or bothering you over new moons or Sabbaths. All these things have at most only a symbolized value: the solid fact is Christ." (Colossians 2:16-17, Phillips Translation)

A third reader may respond to my suggestion about "keep your helmet on" by saying,

"I'm surrounded by temptation—temptations that would put my Christian testimony on the sideline, undermine my relationship to the Lord, and destroy the confidence of my fellow Christians. Do you ever meet temptation? And if you do, can you tell me any way to face it so that I can be a winner? Must I always suffer a concussion when I am tempted? How can I keep my helmet on?"

First, my vocation is as subject to temptation as any

other. I face temptation just like any Christian does, and I sympathize with your problem. I was once asked to come to a Youth Director's conference in the City of Detroit. People were there from all over the city representing every type of institution. They were concerned about a very real problem. They felt that there was so much publicity about pro and college athletes who were moral failures that it was creating a bad example for the young people of America. One of the youth directors in the group came to the defense of all pro athletes and said,

"But don't you think that this is really blown out of all proportion by the loud mouthed sports writers who follow pro athletes? The sports writers are eager to see an athlete step out of line. Then they blow this up far beyond its actual consequence."

Almost everyone in the discussion group seemed to agree with this opinion.

"Yes," they said, "this is it. When athletes step out of line it's highly over-played and not really that bad. Most athletes are morally straight, clean living individuals."

I was the only pro athlete in the room. I just let them talk until almost everyone seemed to be in agreement with the fact that it was the sports writer's fault and not the the immorality of some athletes. Finally, I said,

"Well, I feel that there are relatively more genuine Christians and more clean living people in football than in any other profession. But to say that Christians are in a majority in athletics and to say that immorality is negligible is simply being naive. Christians have always been in the minority and I suppose they always will be. Though there are growing numbers of very fine and dedicated Christian athletes and a lessening amount of immorality among pro athletes, Christians are certainly not in the majority. But then there is no profession in which Christians are in the majority. Yet this is not to discourage us; this is to challenge us. Christians face all types of temptations. Only as we depend upon the Lord and our Christian teammates can we gain strength to be victorious against temptation."

I have noticed that about 75% of the tackles made in a game are made by players who are knocked down or at least off balance. But they are so determined that they make the tackle anyway. When I was a young player I thought that when I got knocked down that this was a good time to rest. I got trampled so many times that I soon learned that the ground was the most dangerous place on the field. So when you get knocked down, get up and go again. Don't stay there. You'll get hurt and you'll miss a great opportunity to be of help to your team. When we sin in thought or deed we can receive immediate forgiveness if we confess it to God. "If we confess our sins He is faithful and just to forgive us our sins." (I John 1:9) I have found that if I confess a sin in the thought stage then it doesn't have a chance to get to the overt stage. If Satan trips you into a temptation, don't stay there—get up and get back into uniform.

Also, don't let him club you with a sin that has already been confessed and forgiven. He will whisper in your ear and say,

"Who are you to serve God? You're the same bird that failed God by. . . ."

Forgiveness is yours if you confessed that sin. So, bounce back immediately into service. Don't let Satan

stop your Christian service by smashing into you with
the memory of sins already forgiven.

"But, Bill," a fourth reader says, "I've kept my helmet
on. I've kept a Christian concern for others in a world
of comparison. I've refused to bow to the legalist. With
the Lord's help I'm waging a fairly successful battle
against temptation. But I'm having difficulty getting the
Christian message across to my friends who don't know
Him. Do other Christians have this problem, or am I just
too timid for the task?"

Let me commend you on your effort to witness for
the Lord. You aren't being overly protective of your
self. You are trying to grasp the right opportunity. A
player who shies away from hard contact is tagged as a
coward. You would say of such a player,

"He's afraid to stick his head in there where it's
rough."

You may already realize that it's not too difficult to
speak at banquets, schools, or church and positionize
yourself for Christ. Now you are learning that it's
toughest to play for Christ in your own league.

The biggest problem that I have in sharing my faith
on the ball club is the idea of players that Christianity
is goodness, rather than relationship to a person. Too
often Jesus Christ is looked upon as someone who is trying to destroy their good time in life. One player asked
me what I did in the off season. I said,

"Well, I just completed my seminary Bachelor of Divinity Degree after going for six consecutive off seasons."

His immediate reaction was, "Well, you know that's
great. Boy, you must be building up a lot of merit points

with God spending all your time going to theological school in the off season. You could make a lot more money doing something else other than that."

I said, "You know, I'm sorry that you've missed it so horribly."

He interrupted, "In what way?"

I said, "I mean that Christianity doesn't have anything to do with building up merit points or doing good things in order to gain favor with God. The only thing that is basically important to God is whether or not you know His son, Jesus Christ, in your heart."

If you can destroy the *works* concept of salvation you are far ahead. Then you can present to your friends an opportunity to come to know the Lord personally.

Most pro football players react affirmatively to genuine Christianity. They are in many cases curious to know what it is to be a Christian. Seldom does anyone say anything or do anything to make it difficult for me to act as a Christian should.

One of Buddy Dial's experiences furnishes a good illustration of the way players in pro football speak for Christ. It was the final day before the first game of the 1963 season. Buddy Parker, then head coach of the Pittsburgh Steelers, called the players together after workout. He said,

"Now, men, it's an important game tomorrow. Give it your best." After encouraging his team, Coach Parker said, "I will see you tonight in the hotel. Is there anything that anyone would like to say before we break up?"

Buddy Dial spoke up and, boy, did this take courage. Buddy was trying to be a Christian influence in a very difficult situation. Buddy later said, as he told me about it, that he just sucked his breath in deeply and blurted out,

"You know it's possible for all of the Catholic boys to go to church on Sunday morning because they have early Mass, but none of the Protestant boys on the team have that opportunity. So I have arranged to rent a room in the hotel and asked one of our Protestant ministers here in the city to come. All of you are invited to come at 10 o'clock in the morning after the pre-game meal. If you would like to come, please feel free to do so."

To Buddy's amazement twenty-five out of the forty players were in attendance that morning, and a great percentage of the coaching staff. This became a regular occurrence for the Pittsburgh Steelers. Every Sunday morning they had a service in which a Protestant minister would speak. The team owner liked it so well that he asked Buddy to bring the Protestant minister along on all the trips. They have continued this practice. Later, Buddy was traded to the Dallas Cowboys, and they've started the same thing there. I think that genuine Christianity, wherever you find it in our society, is reacted to in a favorable way.

Yes sir! Donn Moomaw gave good advice to football players and Christians . . . *Keep your helmet on!*

CHAPTER TEN

Be Obsessed

Our head coach with the Browns has a favorite word of advice to his team. It goes like this—

"Forget the play that went before; it's too late to worry about that. Don't worry about the next play, because that's still in the future. Think only of this play that you're playing now. Concentrate on carrying out the details of your assignment one play at a time."

I often wonder if he got the idea from the Apostle Paul. Paul said,

"Forgetting those things which are behind."

Blanton Collier says, "Forget the play that went before."

Paul said, "This one thing I do."

Blanton says, "Concentrate on carrying out the details of your assignment one play at a time."

Paul says, "This one thing I do . . . I press toward the mark for the prize of the high calling of God in Christ Jesus."

It is as if with body, mind, soul, and everything that he had Paul was pressing for a mark. Paul was like a great track star who is stretching for the finish line. Paul said he was pressing for the finish line in his life.

"This one thing I do. Not these many things I fool around with—but this one goal is mine. I'm pressing for it with everything that is in me with all the power that God supplies."

Paul had a singleness of purpose. This is what has made great track stars down through the centuries. This is what makes great athletes in all sports.

The greatest pass receiver in the history of pro football is Raymond Berry of the Baltimore Colts. He has already bettered Billy Howton's life time record of 503 catches with several years of football still to play. But Raymond Berry is not a man with exceptional ability; actually, Raymond has a lot of physical defects. Compared to other pass receivers he is slow. He has poor vision. He has knee problems. He's always had a bad back. He has everything in the world against his being the great football player that he is. In 1960, when I was still with Detroit, we were playing Baltimore; Raymond had a bad knee. At half time Yale Larry and our other defensive backs were complaining about Berry.

"He's dragging that one leg and still he's killing us."

He caught ten passes that day at half speed with a bad knee. He is the greatest receiver who ever lived—for one reason—because he has a singleness of purpose.

"This one thing I do," says Raymond Berry, "I'm going to be the greatest pass receiver that the world has ever known."

Raymond and I are personal friends and I know he

would never make such a statement aloud; he's much too modest for that. He must have this sort of dedication in his heart, because he works when everybody else rests.

One year at the Pro-Bowl a friend of mine, who played on the Western division team with Berry, said,

"Day after day when everyone else had gone in after the workout, I saw him coming back out. One day I decided that I would watch and see what he was doing. He looked peculiar because he had a net over one shoulder and a ladder over the other and about ten or fifteen little boys tagging along behind. I followed him back out on the practice field. I watched him as he used the ladder to drape the big net over the goal post. He used the goal post as a backstop and he stood in front of the goal post with the net draped over it. Then he had the little boys throw the ball to him. And they threw it to every conceivable position. They'd throw it at ankle height, and then knee height, and on up, and Berry did what he calls the clock drill. He caught the ball at every conceivable position and starting over, he caught the ball at every position going the other way. And then he began to run. He took his running exercises catching the ball at every possible angle."

My friend says that Berry does this almost every day after workout. It's amazing how dedicated Berry really is.

To be obsessed means to be so preoccupied with and totally dedicated to a goal that nothing is as important to you as the attaining of that goal. It's not an accident that Raymond Berry is the greatest pass receiver who ever lived. It is not an accident that he broke Billy Howton's pass receiving record for a career. Raymond Berry is preoccupied with and totally dedicated to the goal of being the greatest pass receiver who ever lived.

The Apostle Paul was obsessed with a bigger and more important goal than athletics. In Philippians 1:12-14 Paul tells us of his obsession. Let me tell you where Paul was when he wrote of his obsession. Paul was in Rome in jail. Paul's friends in Philippi became concerned about him because they loved him dearly. Many of them had been won to Christ personally by Paul. Almost everyone in the church, either directly or indirectly, could count Paul as a dear friend who had made a great spiritual impact upon their life. They decided that they would send one of their own church members to minister to Paul in prison. The messenger's name was Epaphroditus. All the way from Philippi to Rome to see Paul! And how did Paul feel about being locked up? To the amazement of the church at Philippi, to the amazement of Epaphroditus, and to my amazement, Paul—rather than griping and complaining as I might have done—was saying,

"I'm glad to be in jail."

How could Paul be glad to be in jail? How could he be so enthusiastic while in jail? I would have said,

"As long as I was a free man there was something that I could do, but now that I'm in jail what can I do?"

And I would have sulked in the corner, I'm afraid. But not Paul. The more you persecuted him the more effective he became. Paul had been stoned and left for dead, but got up from the dead and continued to speak for Christ. His enemies beat him until he was black and blue, but they could not beat Christ out of him. They laughed and scoffed at him, but they could not ridicule him out of speaking for his Lord. And to throw him in jail was only to broaden his witness. In jail he had an opportunity to talk to Roman soldiers, the cement of the Roman Empire. The army of Rome was that which held the empire together, and if he could influence a Roman soldier he could influence one of the most significant citizens of that day.

The soldiers guarding Paul in Rome were from the Praetorian Guard. They were the elite troops of the Roman army, the emperor's honor legion. They were the very best that the Roman army had. To influence one of the Praetorian Guards, one of the 10,000 soldiers that guarded the emperor, the emperor's palace, the emperor's prisoners, and the emperor's city of Rome, was to influence an important person.

There was a big iron wristlet on Paul's arm and a big iron wristlet on the soldier's arm, and there was a chain connecting the two. And for four long hours that Roman soldier had to listen to every word that Paul had to say. Can't you see the Roman soldier after being chained to Paul. He must have stalked back to his barracks saying,

"That crazy Paul! All he thinks about, writes about, talks about, is Jesus Christ. I get so tired of hearing that name I don't know what to do."

He must have thrown his equipment down on the floor and stomped over to his bunk just cussing mad. That was after the first day of being chained to Paul. But the second day, rather than cussing, his condition could only be described as conviction. The Roman soldiers began to realize that Paul had something authentic, something real that they needed. One after the other the Roman soldiers fell under the convicting power of God's Holy Spirit, and were converted to faith in Jesus Christ.

Not only is it amazing that these Roman soldiers were converted, but they were courageous enough to speak for Jesus Christ in the palace where the emperor lived. You can't really appreciate how courageous this was until you realize that Christianity was beginning to be looked upon by the Roman government as a political party teaching treason. These Christian soldiers became the first missionaries to England. Historians tell us that when part of the Praetorian Guard was transferred to England, Paul's converts among the Guard carried on the Lord's work of spreading the Gospel.

Not only were the Roman soldiers being converted by Paul and becoming witnesses for the Lord, but the Christians in the city of Rome who were formerly ashamed to speak for Christ were gaining courage from Paul's good example. They were now beginning to speak up for the Lord. When these Christians heard about Paul speaking for Christ in jail, they said,

"If he can speak out for the cause in jail, then how much more should we do as free men?"

And so they too began to speak for Christ. They began to come out into the sunlight, on the street corners, and in the market places.

So you see, non-Christians were being converted and Christian people were becoming courageous for their Lord. This to me was revival—and it's revival in any day. But it did not come because of some great orator who came to town to impress everybody with his ability. It came because of a little Jew in jail who was obsessed. He was so obsessed that regardless of what was done to him his mouth could not be shut. He continued to speak for his Lord. And he was highly effective in doing so. This is not only what it took then, but that's what it's going to take today if we're going to be influential in our world for Jesus Christ.

If I'm honest, I must admit that most people are not really obsessed with Jesus Christ. I know a lot of people who are obsessed with athletics. You say,

"Who are you to talk about being obsessed with athletics when you yourself have been playing organized football for over eighteen years—ten years on an amateur basis and over eight years professionally? Who are you to talk about being obsessed with athletics? It seems to me that you like it an awful lot yourself."

And I would agree. I think that football is a wonderful game, and I love all phases of athletics. Nevertheless, football must always be of secondary importance to a Christian. As fine as football is, it isn't worthy of the first place—the obsession place—in your life. Only Jesus Christ deserves the obsession place. Anything else you put there is an unworthy obsession. I feel football is a wonderful platform from which to speak to people, to influence them for good and for God. But if football ever becomes an end in itself, then it has become a false god.

I feel that a lot of other people are obsessed with popularity. Let me be the first to defend popularity. I think that you ought to be as popular as you can. But I think that popularity is a sorry obsession when it becomes your sole reason for living. I get tired of hearing a lot of Christians say,

"The reason that I'm not popular is because I'm a Christian."

I sometimes feel like asking, "Could it be that the reason you're not popular is because you have a rotten personality?"

It could be that God intended for you to be as amiable, as friendly, as kind, and as popular as you possibly could be. It's a cinch you'll never influence anybody towards Christ who doesn't like you. But popularity, as important as it is, is still not worthy of the obsession place in your life. A lot of people have let popularity become their god because all they're thinking about is doing that which pleases the right people to make them more popular.

I also feel that a lot of other people are obsessed with sex. And again, sex in its rightful place is wonderful and beautiful and good. But many people have failed to see that sex is a gift from God, and not a god in itself. When we worship a false god, it always turns into a devil that destroys us and others. It's like the man who goes out in the front yard and digs up a little square of sod. He takes that square of sod into the front living room and shakes it until something falls on the beautiful white carpet. What is it? Dirt! In the front yard it's fine and good, and everybody likes it; but in the front living room on the carpet, it's just plain dirt. There are some things that are wonderful and beautiful and good in their place. In the context of marriage, sex is a gift of God. But out of place and before marriage, just plain dirt. Wrongly used sex hurts the possibility for the happiest marriage that you could look forward to. So it's very important to realize that you have a natural attraction for the opposite sex, and there is nothing wrong with it. God made you that way. Parents, don't ever make your children ashamed of the fact that they're attracted to the opposite sex. Let them realize that God intended that they should channel this natural drive in the right direction so that they can look forward to a happy marriage. So in its rightful place, good; but out of place, dirt.

I think the thing that traps most people today is materialism. People are obsessed with *things*. They are obsessed with money, for example. Money has become their god, and they're money-mad idiots determined to make money. Money is everything to them. Money can do some wonderful things, and money of itself is not bad. It is only when you let money become your god that it is bad. Unworthy obsessions, such as money, are really good when taken in their rightful place. But when made the final obsession of your life, they are in no sense of the word good—they are false gods and therefore bad. Any obsession that replaces Christ is a bad obsession. Jesus urges us to seek God first, and other things will fall into their rightful place in our system of values. Our culture has reversed Jesus' advice—we put secondary values first and relegate God to the last position on the list of things we want.

You say, "All right, Bill, I'll admit that only Jesus Christ deserves the obsession place in my life, and I need to be really obsessed with Him. But let's be practical. How would my life be distinctively different if Christ became my chief obsession?"

To show you the characteristics of being obsessed with Christ let's go back to the Roman prison cell and

watch Paul as he writes a letter to his friends in the
church at Philippi. He is telling his Christian friends that
he has "written off" everything in life that "I may know
Him (Christ), and the power of his resurrection, and
the fellowship of his suffering, being made conformable
unto his death." (Philippians 3:10) Paul wanted above
all else to know Christ. The word *know* is the most
intimate word in the Hebrew language, reserved both
for the most intimate relation between a husband and
wife and man's most meaningful encounter with God.
Paul was determined to know and be known by Christ.

To know Christ intimately is to become obsessed
with Him. I will never give my heart to one I do not
know. Jesus bids me take His cross and follow Him
even to the death. And I am not willing to live and die
for one whom I do not know. Only if I really know
Him am I willing to die for Him. It is not enough just
to believe nice things about Him. I must *know* Him in
my heart, for only as I really know Him can I share
Him with others effectively. I've got to experience Him
in my own heart before I can share Him with anyone
else, or before I can really become obsessed with serving
Him—and serving Him even to death.

Too many people simply know about Him, but don't
really know Him. A coffee salesman was asked,

"How is it that year after year you led the United
States in coffee sales?"

He said, "It's not so hard. I'm sold on it."

When you really get sold on Jesus Christ then you
can sell someone else on Him. But until you really know
Him, you can't get excited about sharing Him with
anyone else. The Scripture says that there'll be many

who come before the Lord in that last day who will say, "Lord, did we not do many wonderful works in your name? Did we not chase out devils in your name?"

And will Jesus say, "Depart from me for I never saw your name on the church roll?"—No!

"Depart from me you wicked for I never *knew* you."

What is really important to Jesus?—that you *know* Him. And if you know Him then you can serve Him like Paul. To know Christ as Paul did is to become obsessed with Him.

In his letter to the church at Philippi, Paul also said that he wanted to know "the power of His resurrection." To experience the same power of God that brought Jesus from the grave is to be given the dynamism of leading a Christ-like life as well as the courage to tell others the good news. I will never be effective in serving Jesus Christ as long as I try to do it in my own power. I must do it in the power of His resurrection.

I've heard some Christians say,

"I'm serving the Lord in my weak way."

And I say the Lord forgive you. Because the Bible says that you're not to serve God in *your weak* way but in *His powerful* way. There is no excuse for your trying to serve God in your strength or in your power; you must serve God in His power. For it says in John 1:12,

"To as many as receive Him to them gave He power to become the sons of God, even to them that believe on His name."

I don't know about you, but these legs of mine are too weak, this body is too frail. I don't have the strength

to run for God in my power. I can only run for God in
God's power. If you try to run in your power, you'll
trip and fall flat on your face. If you'll run in God's
power then all things are possible.

In baring his heart in his letter to the Philippian
church, Paul also said that he wanted to share in the
"fellowship of His (Christ's) suffering, being made conformable unto His (Christ's) death." Though I might
know Him, and though I might have His power in me,
still I must realize that there will be a real possibility of
suffering—of it costing me something. The Scripture
says,

"Yea, and all that will live Godly in Christ-Jesus shall
suffer persecution." (II Tim. 3:12)

If you live godly in Christ Jesus—it doesn't say you
might suffer persecution, it says you *will* suffer persecution. Now this does not mean that somebody is going to
stone you or chop your head off, but it does mean that
it will cost you something. If you really live for Jesus
Christ in an obsessed sort of way, it'll cost you something. Now this does not mean that you should be
obnoxious in your obsession. You should be tactful. It
means that you should be intent, concerned—that you
should really care. You should be obsessed with Him,
and if you are then it will cost you something. And if it
doesn't cost you something, then don't fool yourself—
you're not really obsessed with Him.

This was vividly demonstrated to me in my college
days when I was playing for Baylor University. We had
a boy on our team who was constantly getting one of
his shoulders hurt. This shoulder was always hurting; it
was never right. Before one of our very important

games, he went to the doctor and the coach. He asked them to let him play in the game. He begged them, but they discouraged him again and again. They said,

"We don't think you ought to play in the game because your shoulder is hurt so badly that the only way that you could play is for us to novacaine it. And if we novacained your shoulder, then you could go out there and get hurt and not know it. You could be injured for life and not be aware of it until the novacaine wore off. It's just too dangerous. We can't afford to let you do it."

With tears streaming down his cheeks, he begged the doctor and the coach—practically getting down on his knees to them. Finally, they agreed. They saw that he was not to be denied. They came at him with a big long novacaine needle and began to plunge that shoulder from every direction. They pumped it so full of novacaine that the shoulder was completely deadened. He went into the game with the realization—"I may be injured for the rest of my life, but I want to play in this game worse than I want my shoulder." And right away you might say it "oughta" be against the law to let a player play in a little ole' football game and take a chance on being injured for the rest of his life. And I've heard a lot of people get awfully excited about that—but I'm not going to argue whether it's right or wrong to put novacaine in your body in order to play in a football game. I do say that it's going to take a similar dedication if we're going to be effective in introducing our world to Jesus Christ. We must be willing to sacrifice anything to attain His goal.

To know Christ intimately, to experience the power of God that raised Jesus from the dead, and to share the suffering that comes from being a faithful witness for Christ is to bear with Paul the marks of a Christ-obsessed disciple. To be a Christ-obsessed disciple is to possess these distinguishing characteristics.

CHAPTER ELEVEN

Scout Your Opponent

On Tuesday morning we came in early. We were facing the final week of the season. The pressure was on. We had looked at the films of the St. Louis game in which we had just been beaten two days before. At once we went to work with silent determination to prepare for a victory in this final game. This was a must game. If we won, we would be Eastern division champions for 1964 with a crack at the World's Championship against Baltimore. If we lost—I wouldn't let myself think of that.

The team was now divided. The offense went with Blanton Collier and the other coaches. The defense went with Howard Brinker and Nick Shorich. Nick was telling us,

"Here's what they've got and we know any New York team is tough."

Thus he continued for twenty minutes discussing the personnel. I was thumbing through the thirty-page de-

fensive scouting report which went into even greater
detail. Weights, heights, speeds, weaknesses, strengths,
tendencies, where they went to school, what they were
most likely to do in given situations and in spots on the
field were all there. What they like to do in certain
formations, and their percentages of runs and passes
from certain formations were also included. Howard
Brinker hashed and rehashed the written scouting report
for another thirty minutes.

Finally, the lights went out and we studied films for
another hour. This was a film of the New York Giants
versus the St. Louis Cardinals. We were to see two other
films before the end of the week, spend at least eight
hours of study together, study much on our own, plus
what was to be done on the practice field. All of this is
part of the normal routine of preparation for an important NFL game. We couldn't hope to play well against
any opponent for which we hadn't prepared.

In life we face a very worthy opponent and we,
therefore, need a good scouting report. We need to
know everything that we possibly can about our opponent because he is very real and powerful. The Bible
says that our opponent is like a roaring lion seeking
whom he may devour. The Bible says that our opponent
comes beautifully clothed as an angel of light. He comes
deceptively to hit us in our weakest point. If we under-
estimate the power of our opponent, we're beaten before
we start. For when we think we stand strongest, that is
when we are most likely to fall. Too many people have
underestimated his power because they have heard a
poor scouting report about Satan. He works secretly; in
fact, he doesn't want people to even believe in his exist-

ence. He deceives us, tricks us, and tries to destroy us.

In the third chapter of Genesis we have a very adequate scouting report of Satan. In that first game played in the garden of Eden, we are told exactly what Satan is most likely to do to trick us, to trip us up, to hit us in our weakest point.

He starts out with a really tricky play. In the first verse, we see Satan as he came to the woman and said to her,

"Did God say you could not have the fruit of every tree in the garden?"

And the woman said, "Why, he said we could have the fruit of every tree of the garden but one."

Satan's insinuation is that God doesn't want the woman or Adam to have a good time. Satan implies that God is deliberately withholding some of their happiness.

"Did God say you could not have the fruit of that tree?"

"Oh, we can have the fruit of all the rest of the trees, but not of this tree."

Doesn't the opponent work in the same way today? Doesn't he still tell us that God is some sort of kill-joy, trying to keep us from having a good time? Nothing could be further from the truth. God is the author of all happiness and joy in life, and for us to think that God doesn't want us to have a good time in life is for us to miss completely the teaching of God's word. For the Bible teaches that God is the author of the abundant life and of the happy life. His is the only way to be really happy. Everything that Satan calls joy and happiness in the end brings destruction.

The devil is in the business of taking that which is

pleasurable and making it something miserably ugly. People have so perverted that which is pleasurable, that which brings happiness, that they have run out of things with which to have thrills. So they're playing all kinds of crazy games. I heard about a young man who was playing Russian roulette. The way you play Russian roulette is to put one bullet in a six-shooter and spin the chamber around. There is one chance in six that it will come up even with the firing chamber. And when you pull the trigger there is one chance in six you blow your brains out. Great fun, huh?

People are mixed up on what it is to have a good time. They're playing with dope. Not only adults but even in our junior high schools, high schools, and colleges across America, there are a growing number of those who are becoming addicted to dope and alcohol. One in every sixteen people in the United States today is a problem drinker, people who cannot face life without alcohol. They have no real joy or happiness in life, so they are desperately trying in every mixed-up sort of way to get some artificial joy.

Many teen-agers are being sucked under by Satan's perversion of sex. In marriage sex is good, but sex relations before marriage can hurt your future happiness in married life. At the beginning of the football season we got a new blocking dummy. After workout the coach came over and asked how I liked the new dummy.

"I just love it, coach."

What did I mean by "love"? We throw the word "love" around a lot. I really meant,

"I liked to get my football workout on it."

"I liked to build up my confidence on it."

"I liked to experiment with it."

"I liked to flex my football powers to impress others with it."

You may tell a girl you love her. Don't use love as an excuse. Why don't you be honest and say,

"I'd like to build my confidence on you."

"I'd like to experiment with you."

"I like to flex my sex powers to impress others at your expense."

Yes, you tell her you love her and then you violate her integrity. When you're gone, she stands mauled and spoiled like a worn-out football dummy.

When will we learn? How long will it take? Jesus said, "Seek ye first the kingdom of God and his righteousness and all these other things will be added unto you." But we for 2,000 years have been seeking all these other things and throwing Him the scraps of our lives. Then we wonder why our lives and our world are in a mess. I hope you as the younger generation will learn that God is right. Seek Him first and the other things will be added. But make the mistake of seeking the other things first and you'll find that your lives and your world will become increasingly miserable. The devil is trying to trick people into thinking that if they really follow Christ they won't have a good time. Nothing is a bigger lie.

Our scouting report on Satan in the third chapter of Genesis gives us his second deceptive approach in trying to destroy us. The devil is in the business of tricking people into thinking that God doesn't love them. "The reason that God doesn't want you to eat the fruit of that tree is because he doesn't love you." Isn't this implication ridiculous?

Usually during a game I never notice the crowds, but I remember one blistering hot day in college ball I was sitting on the sidelines breathing oxygen to try to regain my strength to get back into the game. I had to face the crowd to breathe the oxygen. I saw my mother, my brother, my sister, and my sister-in-law only about eight rows up trying to get my attention. My brother, a college coach, was trying to give me signals as to how to play better. He was signalling for me to stay lower, but his eyes quickly left me and returned to the game. My sister-in-law waved sweetly, but was primarily concerned with the ladies' hats and with watching the crowd to see what everybody was wearing. My little sister waved, but she was absorbed in playing with the kids sitting nearby. My mother seemed concerned only about me. Every time I came to the sideline to breathe the oxygen momentarily, I noticed my brother watching the game; my sister-in-law watching the free style show that accompanies most games; my young sister playing with the kids around her; my mother watching me. After about five times of coming out and seeing the same reactions, I realized that my mother couldn't care less about anything but me. She didn't even care whether we won or lost; she was only concerned about me. So I got a little insight into a mother's love. But there is a love that is so much greater than a mother's love, that it is indescribable. Don't ever make the mistake of believing the opponent when he tells you that God doesn't love you. For God's love for you is infinite.

In looking at the game in the garden for the third time, I see that the opponent overpowered the woman in another way.

"The serpent said to the woman, 'Ye shall not surely die!'"

Any good scouting report of Satan should include a warning against the brutally effective, non-deceptive, short yardage power play, the big lie. Nobody believes it will work. But people fell for it then. They fall for it now. And they'll fall for it until time quits. The opponent says,

"Don't even think about it. You've got a long time to live. You're not going to die."

There are nearly three billion people on this globe today and every one of them must die within the next 150 years. People are dying all around us, but we think, "It won't happen to me." Don't believe the opponent when he tells you you're not going to die.

"Well," you ask, "everybody knows that they are going to die, why do you even say that?"

Because, you see, the opponent makes you feel like you've got a long, long time to make your decision for God, and you can make your decision some other day.

He says you can live for God or you can give your best to Christ some other day. But the Bible says "boast not thyself of tomorrow, for thou knowest not what a day may bring forth." The Bible says again that this life is like a vapor. Have you ever seen steam come out of a kettle? It is there for a moment and then it is gone. Your life is like that. The Bible says this life is like the grass of the field which is green and beautiful today, but tomorrow it's gone. Your life is only for a moment. No man is half so foolish as that man who thinks he is going to live for such a long time that he puts important things off until later.

Don't believe Satan when he attempts to get you to postpone your commitment to God by telling you that there is an indefinite future ahead of you in which to give your life to God. Don't believe the enemy when he tells you this terrible lie that you are not going to die.

In the fourth place our scouting report shows that the opponent deliberately told the woman that she did not need God. This was the scoring play.

"Do you know the reason that God doesn't want you to eat of the fruit of that tree? It's because He knows that if you eat of the fruit you will be just like God."

We will never be authorities like God. We must not fall for this old trick of Satan. We are no spiritual authority. Don't try to tell God how to deal with you. Be an humble creature in need of God.

I've seen many spiritual authorities who are always trying to tell God how He's supposed to do things. They say things like this,

"It doesn't make any difference what you believe as long as you're sincere about it."

Sincerity, they say, is the big thing. Why, I once heard about a man who had a habit of running and jumping in bed when he was tired at night. He was out very late one night. When he came in he decided he'd run and jump in bed. He didn't feel like turning on the light and he ran and jumped in what he thought was the bed. But his wife had gone on a house moving spree that day, and he hit on the cedar chest instead. It cost him thirteen stitches in his head. Now he was sincere, but sincerely wrong. The Bible says,

"There is a way that seemeth right unto men, but the end thereof are the ways of death."

Now it may seem right to you that if your pile of goodness is bigger than your pile of badness, that you will make it to heaven. But the Bible says,

"Not by works of righteousness which you have done, but according to His mercy has He saved us."

It doesn't make any difference how good you are. If you don't know Christ, you're lost. It doesn't make any difference how sincere you are; if your sincere faith and trust isn't in Christ and in Him alone, you're lost.

"God helps those who help themselves," you say. A lot of people think that is in the Bible, but it isn't. God didn't say that. The Bible teaches that God helps those who become helpless.

"For by grace are ye saved through faith; and that not of yourselves: it is gift of God not of works, lest any man should boast." (Eph. 2:8, 9)

Benjamin Franklin said that God helps those who help themselves. And though Benjamin Franklin was a good man, I think that I would accept the Scripture as being more authoritative than Ben Franklin.

So you see, you can't come before God as some sort of spiritual authority. You must come as a little child to present yourself humbly before God and ask His forgiveness.

God will not deal with an authority. It means we must have child-like faith—simply trusting in God, not telling God how he's supposed to deal with us. We should come to Him and let Him be the authority and we be the helpless, hopeless sinner who needs Him so desperately. Now if you're trusting in yourself and in your goodness then you're simply that much more lost. You cannot come in your dignity and your conceit.

Christ died for you. All He asks you to do is to commit yourself to Him, and trust Him for what He has done for you already.

Our scouting report tells us to be on the lookout for one other play that the enemy used so well in that first game. Satan still uses this play today. He said to Adam and Eve,

"You have sinned against God. Here comes God, and now you are in trouble. You'd better go and hide."

And doesn't the enemy usually laugh at us when we fail God? He's the one who trips us and causes us to fail God. Then when we do he laughs at us just like he laughed at Judas. The Bible says that Judas came bringing his thirty pieces of silver, and he threw it down on the floor. Judas yelled,

"I have betrayed innocent blood." And the high priest said to Judas, "What's that to us? We don't care."

The devil makes a fool of us. When he's got us in a mess, he just laughs.

"Go and hide, here comes God."

Don't you know that looked ridiculous—Adam and Eve trying to hide behind the trees that God had made? An ostrich has a huge body and a small head. An ostrich sticks his head down in the sand and his huge body is in plain view for everybody else to see. But he thinks himself completely hidden. Adam and Eve hid themselves behind the trees of the garden which the Lord himself had created, and they thought themselves completely out of sight. The Bible says, "If you ascend up into heaven, God is there. If you go down into hell, God is there. If you take the wings of the morning and dwell in the uttermost parts of the sea, God is there."

God is everywhere. God knows your every thought. God knows your every fault. God knows your every action, the things you should have done and the things you have left undone. God knows all about you. So you can't run away from God.

The scouting report tells us not to fall for deceptive moves like, "God doesn't want you to have a good time." God is the author of the abundant life. Satan is the author of unhappiness. "God doesn't love you." Whatever you do don't ever fall for that one. God's love for you is infinitely greater than you could ever imagine. Satan is trying to make you feel that nobody loves you because this makes you dangerously vulnerable to his attacks. "You won't die." Satan tries to get you to postpone any meaningful relationship to God by assuring you that there are an infinite number of tomorrows in which to accept Christ. But, watch for the big scoring play that hits you right in the ego. "You don't need God—you can be just like God." People are trying to be spiritual authorities, trying to tell God how to run His business, and even questioning God's motives and morality. Then when the enemy gets you in a mess, he tells you to run from the only one who can possibly help. "Better hide, here comes God." Don't believe him and let him make a fool of you. In that first game in the garden, he used tricky plays and power plays and scoring plays. He was a tough opponent then. He is a tough opponent now.

You will never defeat this very worthy opponent with your own power. Victory will only come as you trust in God's power. Satan will come at you with his fullback of fear, his quarterback of question, his halfback of halfheartedness, his end of indifference, and his guard of doubt. They will be aligned against you, they'll be running a wedge play against you, and they'll want to run you into the dirt. To make it tougher, up there in the stands will be a whole pep squad of pessimism. They'll be yelling that you can't do it; you don't have a chance; give up; quit; go home; you're going to get beat; you can't win. And you'll feel like quitting except for one thing. Over there on the bench will be a great Coach. This great Coach has never fumbled. He has never been thrown for a loss. He has never called a bad play. He has always won, and He always will win. When this great Coach is on your team and you're on His, and you're together in the game, you can't lose. Every game will be a victory for you.

Date Due

BROADMAN
B P
SUPPLIES

DE 2 1			